THE GREAT SOUTH WOODS
Rambles of an Adirondack Naturalist

Peter V. O'Shea Jr.

THE GREAT SOUTH WOODS
Rambles of an Adirondack Naturalist

ISBN 0-9701516-0-8

Front Cover Photo: *Canada Lynx*, by Gerry Lemmo
Back Cover Photo: *Author at Cedar Lake*, courtesy of Betsy Tisdale

The net proceeds from the sale of this book
will be donated to the
Residents' Committee for the Protection of the Adirondacks.

DEVON PRESS
18 IRVING PLACE
UTICA, NEW YORK 13501

Other books by Peter V. O'Shea Jr.

Guide to Adirondack Trails: Northern Region
Discover the Northern Adirondacks
(with Barbara McMartin, Patricia Collier,
James C. Dawson, Phil Gallos)

Autographed copies of this book
may be obtained from the author:

Peter V. O'Shea, Jr.
P.O. Box 15
Fine, NY 13639

E-mail: PVOSHEA54@hotmail.com

*To my wonderful family, my wife, Maria,
and our children Carmen and Kieran,
the people in my life who have
always made possible my full
enjoyment of the Great South Woods.*

TABLE OF CONTENTS

ACKNOWLEDGMENTS

Many helped and inspired me in my journey through the forest. I am especially grateful to the following:

Red Johnson, recently deceased, one of the last of the old guides, shared freely all his knowledge and competence with me on canoeing and trapping forays on the Oswegatchie.

Clarence Petty gave me a sense of fighting to preserve this magnificent forest. I thank Paul Jamieson for the jewels he put into words in describing the forest. Greenleaf Chase, deceased, was all that a naturalist should be. Among the members of the DEC I have encountered along my way, and who contributed in no small manner in assisting me, the enthusiasm of Terry Perkins and Wayne LaBaff springs instantly to mind. They typify all that is finest in forest rangers. Dick Matzelle and Ken Didion perform the same for the Environmental Conservation officers.

As for those who monitor the trees themselves, the foresters Jim Papero and John Kramer have ever so generously shared their knowledge of the trails and Unit Management Plans with me.

With shepherds like these on the scene, the Great South Woods should still be in good shape as the twenty-first century begins.

Special thanks to Treva Courter who first transformed my manuscript into book form with much affection and helpful suggestions along the way; and to Neal Burdick for his fine, insightful suggestions and editing; without his efforts, this book might never have seen the light of day. A special thank you to Betsy Tisdale, Duncan Cutter, and James Bullard for the generous use of their beautiful photographs. The photos of Gerry Lemmo and Carl Heilman are also appreciated, as is the map of the Great South Woods by Dale Hobson of Hobson's Choice Graphics.

Thanks, too, to Sheila Orlin of Devon Publishing Services for her invaluable assistance and final edit.

The Adirondack Great South Woods
Showing Features Mentioned Prominently in this Book

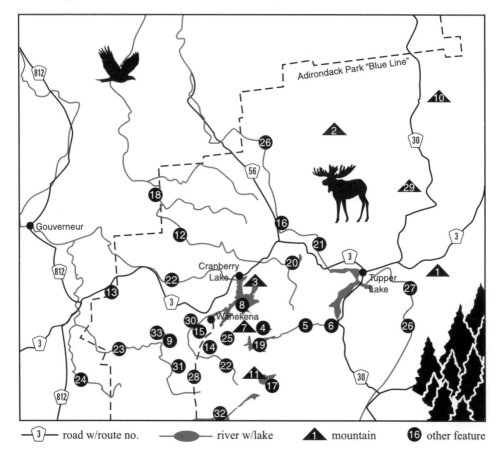

- road w/route no. — river w/lake   ▲ mountain   🔵 other feature

1. Ampersand Mountain	18. Lampson Falls
2. Azure Mountain	19. Lows Lake
3. Bear Mountain	20. Massawepie
4. Big Deer Pond	21. Moody Falls
5. Bog River	22. Oswegatchie River (East Branch)
6. Bog River Falls	23. Oswegatchie River (Middle Branch)
7. Cat Mountain	24. Oswegatchie River (West Branch)
8. Cranberry Lake	25. The Plains
9. Crystal Lake	26. Raquette River
10. DeBar Mountain	27. Raquette River Falls
11. Frederica Mountain	28. Red Horse Trail
12. Grass River (South Branch)	29. St. Regis Mountain
13. Greenwood Falls	30. Sam's Curve
14. High Falls	31. Sand Lake
15. High Rock	32. Stillwater Reservoir
16. Jamestown Falls	33. Streeter Lake
17. Lake Lila	

PREFACE

The Great South Woods—the imagery evoked by the very name connotes many thoughts. The name itself may be an anomaly. After all, for most of the rest of New York State, as well as the Northeast in general, the area defined by the appellation is well to the north.

The term of reference for the name, however, is the fertile, low farm country that is the St. Lawrence Valley. The area was settled just after the turn of the nineteenth century, mostly through subsistence agriculture. These endeavors were supplemented by the establishment of various mills on the area's sundry rivers in order to harness power to process the raw lumber flowing from the great woods to the south.

To the people of the valley, the Great South Woods were where their lumber camps and the deer woods were located. The pursuit of the wily white-tailed deer and the virgin brook trout, complemented by the occasional black bear and lake trout, became a prominent feature of life for the residents of Canton, Potsdam, and other villages in the valley.

The Great South Woods thus assumed an almost mystic bent. Here the normal constraints placed upon people did not prevail; there was neither law nor Sabbath to restrain them in seeking adventure and excitement. This was truly the "frontier," as opposed to the settlements.

For years, a huge glacial erratic (boulder) standing in the town of Colton was supposed to be the line of demarcation between the two different styles of living—the edge, as it were, of the Great South Woods. In the face of a proposal to demolish this boulder in conjunction with road-widening activities in the 1920s, the meaning of this boulder to the local populace and the affection they had for it became readily apparent. A determined effort was inaugurated to prevent heresy. This effort was spearheaded by the now long-defunct *Brooklyn Eagle*, which in itself denotes the importance of the boulder to its adherents. The effort was successful; the boulder was merely moved a short distance to the side of the road. Here it can be seen today in the middle of a very pleasant rest area with a suitably inscribed plaque, detailing its story.

Today the area encompassed by the Great South Woods extends roughly across those parts of St. Lawrence, Franklin, and Lewis Counties that are in the Adirondack Park. It also includes the northern parts of Hamilton and Herkimer Counties and is usually considered to extend to the towns of Russell, Edwards, and Pierrepont just north of the Adirondack Park in St. Lawrence County. Within it are several rivers that drain the Adirondacks in a northerly direction: the Deer, Oswegatchie, Grass, Raquette, and St. Regis, plus the Beaver and Bog, which flow west and east, respectively.

This is demonstrably the most remote and unknown part of the Adirondacks and the area where the old ways have lingered longest.

A considerable amount of focus has been put on the area recently with a proposal to establish the premier wilderness area east of the Mississippi River—the Bob Marshall Wilderness, along with an allied proposal to establish a Boreal Reserve consisting of an untrammeled area of northern conifers. Both depend on the sprawling undeveloped forests that still exist locally.

So extensive and relatively pristine is this remnant wild land that it has been proposed by a variety of scientists as the area for restoring the so-called "extirpated megafauna" to the Adirondacks. Some of these "extirpated megafauna" seem to have recognized the area's potential on their own, as will be seen in the chapter entitled "Creatures of the Shadow."

I began my acquaintance with the Great South Woods while doing fieldwork for the book *Guide to Trails of the Adirondacks: Northern Region*, published by the Adirondack Mountain Club (ADK). My knowledge of and love for the area deepened considerably as I co-authored several other regional guides and participated in the official Breeding Bird and Herptile Surveys of New York State. I was one of the relatively few compilers for the latter two surveys in this relatively unknown part of the Adirondacks.

Hunting and fishing spurred my initial love of this unique and spectacular area and were the catalysts in broadening both my knowledge and affection for these very special woods. I employed a more holistic approach and eventually became a field naturalist at the Indian Creek Nature Center in St. Lawrence County. Much of what I recount here stems from personal observations in walking the woods, as well as from regular appearances as a guest naturalist at the Adirondack Visitor Interpretive Centers (VIC), located at Paul Smiths and Newcomb.

I arrived in these woods after a lengthy, rather indirect odyssey of searching. It all began in Flushing, New York, in the 1940s. Flushing was then in the process of rapidly changing from a suburban to an urban landscape. All that remained to evoke images of a bygone era was the "Big Woods" surrounding Queens College. There I became acquainted with ring-necked pheasants, cottontail rabbits, and a mysterious creature whose existence was only rumored, the opossum. Shortly after I confirmed the possum's existence, the woods were demolished in order to accommodate the expansion of Queens College, and I moved on.

The woodlands and abandoned farmland of Schoharie County were next in my quest. Here I became acquainted with deer and red fox for the first time and also witnessed the beginning of an "invasion" that would bring wild turkey and coyote into Schoharie's woodlands. This was not the only invasion here, however. Second homes were beginning to proliferate over the landscape and, although I originally went there for that reason, I moved on again. The purple lilacs and the day lilies blooming in the midst of the woodlands where they had been long ago planted by a housewife became as much a part of the past as the flowering dogwood that once bloomed in the old "Big Woods" of Flushing. My father retired to Schoharie County and from him I received a number of reports of black bear spreading into that county where they had not been seen for well over a century.

The wind-swept, snow-laden Tug Hill Plateau was the next step in my odyssey. Here I purchased 737 acres on the very top, in the town of Montague, and proceeded to initiate my very own private conservation efforts. I had five wildlife ponds constructed through the Soil Conservation Service and set about reforesting ninety abandoned farm acres into conifer plantations. Some of the latter was done manually, with a mattock, as my back could attest to at the time. For these endeavors I received a plaque naming me the Lewis County Conservationist of the Year in 1974.

At this juncture in my odyssey I believed fervently that private initiative was the sole way to protect the environment. I adamantly opposed the Bond Act of 1972 and was not hesitant to state as much.

Despite my best efforts, my attempts at preserving the natural landscape came to naught. Some of those who owned surrounding acreage did not look on preserving their lands as forest and wetlands as meaningful and proceeded to sell lots for development. My taxes skyrocketed in spite of my own efforts at trying to offset them by cutting pulpwood, planting potatoes for sale, etc.

Sadly, I concluded that private efforts alone could not even begin to protect our environment and natural landscape. I underwent a metamorphosis of sorts and became an avid proponent of state ownership of public lands to preserve our natural environment. A total transformation! In accord with this new conviction, during the intervening years I have been on the Region 6 Open Space Committee, the St. Lawrence County Environmental Management Council and the board of directors of the fledgling Residents' Committee for the Protection of the Adirondacks. I have also been conservation chair for a number of environmental groups.

The primary area of concern of this book is the flora and fauna of the Great South Woods. In addition, I describe some of the natural gems I have encountered in my travels here—mountains, rivers, lakes, and waterfalls to name a few. A number of the trails described in the field guides I have authored lead to some of these. I add human dimension by recalling some of the more memorable folks of the forest I have encountered along the trails and elsewhere. Mostly, however, the book dwells on wildlife. This is primarily because I feel wildlife is the main factor which elevates this part of the Adirondacks and bestows upon it a special aura.

I have dwelt in some depth on the fauna royal—predators, megafauna, and the alleged extirpated species. Neither is the avian life that makes the Great South Woods so special neglected. Here we have boreal birds, raptors and such. Finally, even more mundane forms of fauna are not neglected; there is a place for herptiles and biting insects in these pages.

Wherever possible, I have sought to impart a personal perspective, in the hope that it might enhance the discussion. I feel especially fortunate and blessed at some of the wonders I have witnessed. What is recounted here is the result of lengthy observing and seeking in the Great South Woods. This is above all an attempt to share with others some of that joy and sense of wonder that the Great South Woods has never ceased to furnish me.

From all of the above, but especially from tramping through the forest, always searching and seeking, has come the knowledge imparted in this book. With my past life as a Sergeant in the New York City Police Department probably being the frame of reference, a reviewer of my first trail guide stated that I had progressed from "walking a beat to walking the big woods." I guess I have.

FOREWORD

My first acquaintance with Peter O'Shea occurred almost twenty-five years ago. I had corresponded with him through the mail when he joined a small "grassroots" organization that started in the Canton/ Potsdam area. The name of the organization was "Citizens to Save the Adirondack Park," and it was formed to oppose the plans of the Horizon Corporation to establish a huge second home development in the middle of a relatively wild part of the Adirondacks' northwest quarter. The plan envisioned an airport, golf course, several ponds made by dams on an important trout stream, and hundreds of buildings, all at the expense of a destroyed forest resources area.

We were pleased to have Peter's help in opposing this ill-conceived plan. It was several years later that I actually met him, as we both pursued a similar approach to protecting that crown jewel of the state, the Adirondack Park.

Who would have thought that a member of New York City's Police Department, operating in one of the word's largest metropolitan areas, would retire to pursue a career in the woods?

Peter is a self-taught zoologist, botanist, plant pathologist, and wildlife observer who has spent enough time examining the North Country's life forms that he is well qualified to convey his experience of a "hands-on" approach to those who choose to read this book.

While the reader may not agree with all of his conclusions, I hope that his remarks will stimulate others to take the time to study the complex relationship that exists between the many plant, animal, and bird populations of the North Country of which Peter's "South Woods" is a part.

If the book encourages others to investigate the wonders that are often ignored in our regimented rush for a better life, Peter O'Shea's efforts will have been rewarded.

—Clarence Petty
Potsdam, New York

I

CHARISMATIC WILDLIFE

Bull Moose

Wildlife of a truly spectacular nature, the result of size, form or some other defining aspect, are fauna that can convey a sense of thrill or trepidation. They also convey a sense of excitement that is all too rare nowadays when most encounters are with more prosaic wildlife in a mundane setting. These charismatic wildlife species have their stronghold in the vast wilderness of the Great South Woods and the corresponding spectacular background adds to the thrill and excitement of each encounter. For these creatures of charisma are in general quite leery of humankind and, hence, likely to be found where evidence of their presence is least in abundance. The wilderness areas of the Great South Woods qualify eminently in this respect.

Bear, bobcat, and fisher are among those creatures who depend on the vast expanse of untrammeled forest present here. For others, such as moose and marten, it is the boreal nature of that forest that serves as the prime attraction. Otters depend on the wild shorelines and unpolluted waters so much in evidence in the Great South Woods.

While I occasionally enjoy the actual sighting of these creatures, it is the mere fact of knowing they are present that adds zest to daily living in the North Country. For, as the eminent wildlife scholar, Aldo Leopold, was once quoted as saying, "The excellence of wildlife is the hallmark of quality in a wilderness." In this hallmark of quality the Great South Woods are without peer!

MEGAFAUNA

These are remnants of a bygone era now so remote that they barely linger as a dim memory in the subconscious of those alive today. The wildlife at the time of the glaciers' recession and the entrance of man into North America was truly awesome. The sight of the charismatic megafauna, as the vast assemblages of large mammals were called, is rivaled only by that of the Serengeti Plains in Africa today.

Alas, today in the Adirondacks they are mostly gone and have been for 10,000 years or so. A growing number of scientists feel it was the entrance of man with his sophisticated weaponry that lead to their demise.

Two members of our modern fauna qualify as "charismatic megafauna" using the criterium of five-hundred-pound body weight as a minimum standard. Moose and black bear somehow escaped that long-ago carnage and grace our modern landscape. Their survival probably resulted mainly from their being solitary creatures as opposed to their being members of the more vulnerable herds that were all eliminated.

BLACK BEAR

The black bear has had an intimate and historical association with the Adirondacks stretching from the popular writings of Charles Dudley Warner in the middle of the nineteenth century to the present day. Populations of this large omnivore are near optimum in the Great South Woods.

Hikers and campers in the forests of the Great South Woods have had a close if rather strained relationship with the black bear. This is particularly true around the campsite at night. It is well known locally that if there is any food available bears will find it. Often the persistence of bruin when seeking nutrition around the nocturnal campfire verges on aggressiveness. Tying the food up securely out of the reach of the earnest marauder is the only way to foil its efforts. I vividly recall being awakened at 3:00 A.M. one morning, in my pup tent on a bank of the Oswegatchie, by a creature that had almost knocked the tent completely over. When I hollered, "What are you doing?" rather inanely considering the circumstances, the bear, for such it was, took off for parts unknown. Much to my relief, of course, albeit the incident was enough to keep me awake until I rose at the crack of dawn.

In similar fashion, sightseers would head nightly for years to the small public dumps once maintained by the local towns in hopes of gaining a glimpse of what was until recently the sole surviving member of the megafauna in the Adirondacks. This covert feeding of bears was tacitly encouraged by resort owners and others in an attempt to provide amusement for tourists. I once saw twenty-three bears feeding together contentedly at the old Cranberry Lake Dump. This extra supply of protein for bruin came to an abrupt end with the state-mandated closure of these local dumps. I often find myself speculating as to what effect this loss of extra nutrition will eventually have on the overall population of black bears.

Bears in the Great South Woods can occasionally attain a prodigious weight. Bears over 750 pounds live-weight have been documented near both Tupper Lake and Cranberry Lake. I attribute this mammoth size to the extensive wilderness areas, which give bears an even chance of living a life uninterrupted by the bullets of human marksmen. And, of course, growing all the while during the living.

Bears begin to enter hibernation in late November. Females with cubs are the first to enter hibernation with the actual date varying with weather conditions. In the mild December of 1994, bears were around and about until the end of the month. I saw tracks that year until the first week of January. In any event there is usually a frenzied feeding orgy immediately prior to hibernation. Bears gorge themselves on beechnuts and black cherry mast, climbing trees if need be to secure them. When these are not available they will often go north to the St. Lawrence Valley to obtain food sources not readily available in the Great South Woods, including pollen and honey from beehives and the standing corn in the fields of the valley. It is on these occasions that we get the unusual and much cherished sightings of bears at Indian Creek Nature Center near Canton.

The den sites themselves are often in blowdowns or at the base of large trees or snags. Some excavating is done, but most of the cover results from the build-up of snow. Contrary to popular belief, caves are rarely used for denning.

Bears eat berries and fruit of all kinds with gusto during the summer. Red raspberry patches are often entirely demolished by feeding bears when the shrub is in fruit. Shadberry trees are simply knocked over for the fruit. I find shadberry the sweetest of all, but almost impossible to obtain due to the depredation of bears!

The leaves of clintonia are especially relished in spring, as are the roots of trout lily. A treasured memory is following a feeding bear for over a mile as it dug up the roots of the recently withered trout lily along the old Dobson Trail. A turn of a curve and the sight of a fleeing rump was enough to furnish a memory for a lifetime in this instance.

Carrion, too, is avidly sought after by black bears, particularly when emerging from hibernation, usually in April. An unusual occurrence happened on the Irish Hill Road in the town of Fine in connection with this propensity of black bears. A power line had fallen during a heavy storm and electrocuted a white-tailed deer that had come in contact with it. Along came a hungry bear who, being true to its tribe's penchant for carrion, commenced to feed on the deer. It, too, was electrocuted almost immediately. A phone call from a friend enabled me to view the two carcasses before they were removed by the Town Highway Department.

There are reputedly around 4,000 black bears in the Adirondack Park. Traffic fatalities account for only a few deaths every year and the legally allotted harvest under the auspices of the Department of Environmental Conservation (DEC) seems reasonable for the present despite the too-lengthy season. A threat could loom on the horizon, however. This threat springs from the inordinate prices paid for bear gall bladders in the Orient as both an aphrodisiac and a medicinal herb. This has led to illicit poaching rings in other areas of the Northeast and I have recently seen signs that have led me to surmise that poaching could be working its way toward us. This could be devastating on bear populations, especially if dogs are legalized in the hunting of bear.

Let us hope that this potential threat never materializes. Instead, may some future author of note be singing the praises of the Adirondack black bear at the end of the twenty-first century as Charles Dudley Warner was extolling it in the middle of the nineteenth.

MOOSE

His majesty the moose, the ultimate in Adirondack megafauna, was once the monarch of the Great South Woods. What more need be said of this regal cervid that seems to be ever so slowly re-colonizing its former domain?

Moose began to appear regularly in the Great South Woods around 1980, coming initially as wanderers from occupied habitat in New England to the east and apparently in lesser numbers from Canada to the north. Their recovery is hampered and prolonged because they are coming into the Adirondacks from different directions and also by the fact that there is a skewed sex ratio in favor of males because it is bull moose that have the most marked tendency to wander, especially during the rut in September and October.

Recognizing this fact, the DEC commenced a series of public hearings in the early 1990s to decide whether or not to import a number of cow moose from out of state. I attended one such hearing in Canton and the opinions clearly were in favor of the re-introduction program. Nevertheless, the DEC ultimately decided against the restoration, citing a strong minority opposition expressed in one or two other hearings. Many eyebrows were raised at what seemed a typical bureaucratic decision. Conservationists and environmentalists both take solace in the fact that the moose, for the present at least, seems to be undertaking its own restoration, albeit at a far slower pace than most would favor.

Moose have to meet and find congeners (members of their own genus) for successful mating to occur! And, needless to say, the presence of one gender alone will not ensure an ultimate viable population of moose.

While wandering moose may put in a brief appearance anywhere in the North Country, pockets of population concentrations appear sparse. Two have been pinpointed. One is in the vicinity of Owl's Head Mountain and Meacham Lake in the northern Adirondacks, while the other is near Speculator in the south. Both consist of a relatively few loosely affiliated animals but the hope is that these two small concentrations will eventually be the nuclei for moose repopulating the entire Adirondack Park.

Cows with twin calves have been observed on several occasions, especially on the Moose River Plains. As of 1999 there were approximately one hundred moose in the North Country of New York. Almost all are in the Adirondacks although a few are in the St. Lawrence Valley just north of the Great South Woods.

Several trends have become evident regarding the moose in the Great South Woods. Beaver ponds appear to be the habitat of preference rather than the boreal peatlands so often depicted elsewhere as the idyllic representation of typical moose abode. Streams often appear to be followed by our resident moose; one radio-collared bull near Saranac Lake spent an entire winter following various stream courses. Another radio-collared bull left the Adirondacks to go north to the edge of the St. Lawrence Valley in search of a mate during the rutting season in 1995. It then retraced its path almost in the exact same footsteps after the rut had concluded. I saw its tracks coming and going just outside the hamlet of Cranberry Lake.

Moose also seem to be showing an inordinate fondness for road salt and trek here from a wide surrounding area in winter in order to obtain the salt washed from the highway. At least one area, near Meacham Lake, has achieved a measure of local fame by furnishing a regular moose lick adjacent to a state highway. This is much the same reason why moose resort to beaver ponds in summer. The aquatic vegetation, including both yellow and white water lilies, is unusually high in sodium, an intrinsic part of the nutrients they apparently must have in their diet.

Another spectacle is the sight of moose cavorting with Holstein and other dairy cows. Much has been written concerning the tendency of the 1,300-pound radio-collared bull, "Big Richard," to engage in this. The explanation is not in the least complex—there simply is currently a lack of cow moose in the Great South Woods. So roaming bulls with "the humor on" them resort to what in their eyes is the next best thing!

From what I have seen, moose seem to be feeding heavily on balsam fir and quaking aspen. The latter had been fed on so heavily at the edge of the "Plains" south of Cranberry Lake one winter that the area in question looked like it had been a corral! Twice I have seen where bulls in rut have thrashed small trees, in both cases a striped maple (or "moosewood"). This is also the tree of preference for the white-tailed bucks in rut in the Great South Woods.

It was September 1984 and I was on the highway between Long Lake and Tupper Lake. Two huge, black bovine-like creatures crossed in front of my vehicle and entered the adjacent forest by jumping the short Department of Transportation (DOT) barrier at roadside. One weighed half a ton; the other was the size of the largest white-tailed buck I had ever laid eyes on. I knew instinctively—a cow moose and her calf of the year. Their gait was very similar to that of a horse at the trotters. My memory of the two creatures is still vibrant. It is a sight I hope to see again soon and one I wish fervently will be available sooner rather than later for all in the Great South Woods to enjoy!

PREDATORS

These are the creatures that receive their sustenance from the flesh of other creatures. It is perhaps the ultimate in excitement to gain a fleeting glimpse of one of these furtive prowlers of the forest. Merely knowing they are in the vicinity suffices to impart a feeling that things are right with the world. A more intimate knowledge can be gleaned from tracks in snow and mud, sites of occasional kills, and the very occasional piercing shriek from the forest depths.

All their senses are fine-tuned to perfection. Their lethal instruments for the dispatching of prey are also honed to the highest degree. According to nature's dictates they must be far sparser in number than the quarry they seek. This scarcity, along with the sharpening of the senses, combines to make an actual sighting of one of these forest princes an event to be treasured forever.

The Great South Woods hosts a lengthy list of these magnificent creatures. Indeed it is the refuge of last resort for several who have virtually disappeared from the rest of the state.

BOBCAT

It was just after dusk and I was trodding back to camp in the snowy woodlands of Lewis County. Suddenly a yowl, so fierce that it prompted shivers all along my spine from my skull to my waist, emanated from the blackness of the forest. I knew instinctively that it was the February mating cries of a bobcat, but that did little to allay my anxiety. Recalling that I was at least five miles away from the nearest fellow human, I made the trip back to camp as fast as my snowshoes would carry me.

The bobcat is relatively abundant in the Great South Woods since almost the entire forest is suitable habitat for them. Studies conducted recently, in connection with Lloyd Fox's master's thesis at the SUNY College of Environmental Science and Forestry Wildlife Forest at Newcomb, disclosed that bobcats in the Adirondacks have a much larger home range than those in the Catskills. They are as abundant as they are due to the fact that their habitat still exists here rather than to any intrinsic quality of that habitat.

These findings caused a considerable stir in the wildlife community when they were published. Lloyd subsequently moved on to Kansas but his theory has proven itself correct over the ensuing years.

Their abundance contrasts starkly with the sparseness of reported sightings. Felines in general appear to possess a proclivity for staying invisible when they desire to, which is most of the time. Another example of this is the larger, long-tailed "cat-of-the-shadows"—the panther—which possesses such furtiveness that its very existence is denied by officialdom.

Locally, bobcats reach a greater size than elsewhere in the state. Dick Matzelle, a DEC conservation officer in the area, regularly gets cats turned in to him for tagging that are in excess of forty pounds.

Some are almost fifty pounds! So large are local bobcats that some scientists consider them to belong to the sub-species "gigas," which is prevalent north of the U.S./Canadian border. Bobcats of the Great South Woods have to be larger than average for in most winters they have to kill deer to survive. They usually do this by furtively approaching a reclining deer on its "bed" and dispatching the deer with bites and blows to the neck region. Bobcats prey on live deer as well as carrion in the vast deer yards of this area.

Bobcats supplement their fare of venison in the winter by preying also on that all-around staple, the snowshoe hare. I once saw tracks of bobcat and lynx in the same area on consecutive days in Peavine Swamp in the town of Clifton. They were certainly feeding on hare, as deer are usually quite rare in Peavine Swamp in winter.

On another memorable occasion I heard the bobcat render a different sort of vocalization while I was skiing on the old railroad bed from Sabbatis into Lake Lila. A snowshoe hare, the picture of terror, darted across the tracks not one hundred feet in front of my skis, pursued closely by a large bobcat in keen anticipation of a meal. Approximately three minutes later a shrill scream of a sort I had not heard before came from the vicinity of the conifer patch where the cat went after the hare. I knew of course from what source the scream emanated as I had personal knowledge, so to speak, of the players in the drama. I wondered in my own fashion if some of the old-time guides were actually as knowledgeable woods-wise as people seemed to think they were. So I reproduced the sound as best I could and asked Red Johnson of Fargo to identify it. He did, without pausing in the slightest.

I learned two things from the above incident. The first was that the old guides did indeed possess an intimate knowledge of the forest that is virtually unattainable today. The second was that my cup of joy would come nowhere near to running over if the bobcat were ever to disappear from its forest home in the Great South Woods.

RED FOX

The red fox has been elegantly described as the "prancing prince of the moonlight." Anyone who has been graced with a glimpse of this royal cardinal-colored canine as he delicately treads through the forest will testify to the aptness of this description.

I usually see one or two red foxes a year while hiking in the forest. I find them far less wary than coyote, who I usually see only from a moving vehicle.

Breeding begins in late winter and from that time onward tracks in the snow are usually paired. Yapping barks are usually heard at this time also and continue while the pups are being weaned. Birth in our area is usually in April. I often find dens in conifer plantations, but abandoned fields and openings are also often utilized. The den is usually dug into a slight rise or hillock when the soil is loose and the digging easy.

There is considerable evidence that the appearance of the Eastern coyote in the Great South Woods has had a depressing effect on populations of red fox. In the past few years there has been an observed tendency for red fox to be seen around villages in the Adirondacks. I found one den right on the outskirts of the hamlet of Cranberry Lake. There is no doubt in my mind that this latest development is in direct response to harassment from the larger coyote, who is usually more loathe to go into hamlets (although not always).

Red fox, like other canids, feed heavily on fruit from July to October, beginning with red raspberry, then blueberry, blackberry, and finally black cherry. One fox developed the habit of coming up to cars to be fed on the Horseshoe Lake Road when the Veterans' Memorial Camp was in operation. People regularly fed black bears along this road and this enterprising fox got into the act, though not when the bears were present.

Come late summer red fox flock to the grassy roadsides flanking the area's highways. There they feast on grasshoppers and crickets to their hearts' content. Mostly it is the young ones who are seen here— they have not yet developed total sophistication. Meadow voles are also common here and foxes delight in pouncing on them. They do this by leaping in the air and descending on the hapless prey with all four feet. This is especially notable when a thin layer of snow lies on the ground. A truly entrancing spectacle is then presented for the pleasure of a fortunate observer.

How much of the Great South Woods would still be the same if the above sights were to disappear?

EASTERN COYOTE

It has been said that the Eastern coyote is an enigma wrapped in a puzzle. This results both from the history of the creature's actual tenure in the Great South Woods and from doubt revolving around its genetic background. In the latter issue both dogs and wolves have been implicated by some as being a component of this large canid's pedigree. In the former, the view has recently been put forth that the Eastern coyote has always had a presence in the Adirondacks. This is in sharp contrast to the prevailing thesis that these canids spread into our area from adjoining Canada beginning in the 1920s. What is the actual situation?

There is no doubt that when coyotes first entered the region there were occasional matings with free-running dogs from which resultant hybrids emerged. I recall seeing some of these "coy dogs" three decades ago. They were truly fantastic looking creatures that defied categorization. Some were quite large but in all that I saw the dog strain clearly shone through. I recall noting one labeled a "dogote" at the old Conservation Department's zoo at Delmar outside Albany. No more outlandish looking creature could be conjured forth!

All this intermingling apparently occurred because of a lack of suitable mates for the colonizing coyotes. These canids now breed true and no longer are hybrids seen. The hybrids that once existed did not successfully pass along their genes due to a breeding time phase inconsistency with full-blooded coyotes. The animals we see today have very few if any dog genes in their composition.

Wolf genes are another matter. This is a distinct possibility, indeed a probability! The Algonquin wolf in southern Ontario and Quebec has been revealed to have coyote DNA among its genes that could only have resulted from hybridization at some time in the distant past. The reverse situation will also prove true, I'm sure, when genetic tests are ultimately performed on the Eastern coyote.

This introgression of wolf genes I'm certain has proven a boon to the Eastern coyote in its conquering of the Great South Woods. It has made it much easier for it to dispatch deer. And dispatch deer the Eastern coyote does particularly in winter and when fawn are in evidence during the late spring. Packs are formed solely for this reason. Even in packs, however, the Eastern coyote proves elusive and is primarily recognized by the sounds the pack makes rather than by actual sightings.

Eastern coyotes begin a varied range of vocalizations, usually starting in August. These range from yips and yaps to barks and even occasionally a howl that is almost, but not quite, wolf-like. These sounds serve to keep the pack in touch and also, probably, to stimulate hunting. The young of the year start going on their own in August and at this time frequently are sighted along roadsides hunting for mice and insects.

Most of the dens I have observed are on the banks of creeks or other water bodies. Ridges are often used, particularly the sandy gravels that have been left behind by the glaciers in the form of eskers. I remember fondly one natal den that stood for years on the banks of the Oswegatchie River just below High Rock. The hordes of canoeists and hikers who camped and lunched at this popular spot on the river were blissfully unaware of what was transpiring a mere stone's throw from them!

I have not heard any conclusive proof of any incident of coyotes attacking people in the Great South Woods. Several close friends related instances to me of the canids "curling their lips" at them and I believe this to be true. There have also been recorded, though rare, instances of the Eastern coyote entering some of the smaller hamlets and preying on house cats.

Much more common fare is fruit and beechnuts starting in mid-summer. From this time until the appearance of snow upon the ground, mast provides a major component of the Eastern coyote's menu.

With the onset of winter, things change. White-tailed deer supplemented by snowshoe hare now become the main prey. Packs form and are almost indispensable in deer predation. I say almost because I have noted on two occasions large Eastern coyotes hunting deer solo. I did not see the outcome of these chases, but as these canids can attain a weight of sixty pounds locally, I can well imagine one of this size taking down a deer by himself.

I feel coyote did in fact enter the Great South Woods from Canada and in the short time they have been here have established themselves as the main predator. That is not to say they have usurped the role of the Eastern timber wolf. The latter canid preys on deer year-round rather than being restricted to the fawning and the winter season. This has major implications for the ecology of the entire ecosystem, one the Eastern coyote cannot quite provide! However, I believe there currently is a niche for both of them in the Great South Woods and the Adirondack Park in general.

I anxiously look forward to the day both are present in viable numbers to perform their allotted role in the ecosystem of the Great South Woods!

FISHER

With this glorious member of the mustelid clan we come to a predator whose numbers approach the maximum possible in the Great South Woods. The fisher has long been associated with old-growth forest in the Adirondacks, but lately it has spread into early successional forests while at the same time expanding its range into the St. Lawrence Valley. Its tracks can regularly be seen in the snow at Indian Creek Nature Center near Canton.

It was not always thus. Fisher numbers declined dramatically in the 1920s mainly due to the pressure of unregulated trapping. And trappers do seek out the fisher, particularly the more fine-furred female whose pelt is much relished on the fur market. As fisher females are considerably smaller than males, trappers can concentrate on them to the ultimate detriment of the entire population.

I recall a warm October day in the 1970s when New York State was paying $250 for live-trapped fisher for translocation to the Catskills to establish a population there. A friend had one in what he felt was a secure cage made of solid lumber. Elation overcame him as he contemplated the funds he would receive from the state of New York for his quarry. In celebration he stopped off to imbibe at a local tavern; upon exiting from same he found the fisher and his $250 both gone. The fisher had chewed a hole through the 2x4s and left on the wind. So much for easy money and the physical prowess of a fisher!

I often see fisher abroad in the winter. At this time they hunt both day and night in order to obtain sufficient nutrients to survive. A number have stood up and stared when they saw me, much as a woodchuck will do, but the majority make a quick exit without so much as a backward glance.

Snowshoe hare are favored prey in winter, along with the occasional porcupine. Often a fisher will climb a tree to take a porcupine. The prey is dispatched by repeated bites to the facial area while staying away from the porcupine quills. After partaking of the feast, the fisher turns the porcupine's skin completely inside out. This is a sure sign of a fisher kill.

Fisher utilize temporary snow dens for shelter in winter. Natal dens are almost always a hole high up in a hollow tree. Standing snags are important in this respect and as far as the fisher is concerned there never can be enough of them spread through the forest.

Fisher frequently kill raccoons and skunks also. The former is a formidable scrapper himself, but no match for this ferocious mustelid, while the spray of the latter appears to be no deterrent at all as far as the fisher is concerned. Old-timers in the town of Fine refer to the virtual elimination of skunk when the fisher put in an appearance there around mid-century. Fisher also relish soft mast and beechnuts in season, as do all the predators of the Great South Woods with the exception of the feline tribe. Mountain ash berries seem to be a favorite provider of soft mast.

An interesting observation is the near unanimous opinion of trappers locally that the much-vaunted ferocity of the fisher is not much in evidence where humans are concerned. They state that this is in marked contrast to the mink, which is a compressed bundle of fury when taken in a trap. Another hallowed tradition that does not hold up under scrutiny is the alleged fondness of the fisher for water. While it often hunts along streams and lakeshores, it shows a decided aversion to actually entering the water. On a number of occasions I have noted signs in the snow where a fisher crossed over a tiny rivulet on the flimsiest of alder branches rather than get its feet marginally wet!

Adirondack fisher can be transferred to other areas, but to my way of thinking, the fisher remains the emblem of the spirit of the Great South Woods!

MARTEN

The marten and the fisher stand together in my mind as two glorious mustelids of the big green woods. Populations of both are as high in the Great South Woods as they are anywhere in the "Lower 48."

Marten numbers declined precipitously in the 1930s as was the case with the fisher. Until quite recently marten were believed to be absent from the Great South Woods. I recall, vividly, the DEC making a proposal to the Citizens' Advisory Committee of the Five Ponds Wilderness Unit Management Plan advocating the re-introduction of marten to the Five Ponds Wilderness. This was in 1982 and I also vividly recall the "knowing" looks of the old-time sportsmen and guides who were on the committee. They knew that marten were present and had been for quite a while.

The first marten I set eyes on was lying dead in a 220 conibear trap. The animal had been inadvertently taken by a friend trapping fisher in the Five Ponds Wilderness. Subsequently I saw a live one exiting from the attic of a two-story camp on the South Branch of the Grass River. I then knew for certain that marten were definitely here and that once again the official pundits were incorrect in their assessment of the status of a creature in the Great South Woods.

Since then I have seen close to a dozen marten in the wild, with only one of them in the trees. Quite often marten come to lean-tos, especially in the High Peaks, where they are attracted to an abundant and relatively free food supply. Jellies and jams seem to be particularly treasured! My two children, in fact, saw a marten on a trek up Phelps Mountain. And this before their father, the "woodsman," had been fortunate enough to spy one!

Mike Virkler is an old-time woodsman who had a hunting camp in what is now the Watson's East Wild Forest. I have cherished memories of time spent there over a decade ago. One of the most prominent of these memories was the thrill of seeing no fewer than three marten at once coming to feed at the scraps pantry that Mike had assembled at the camp for them. Carcasses, bread, fruit—they relished it all and repaid it with sights that were a thrill of a lifetime!

Snags and holes in hollow trees are used for the natal den site, but I often see martens using downed trees also. Horizontal logs lying crisscross across the lay of the land are quite common in old-growth forests and furnish food as well as cover for the marten. For this mustelid relishes red-backed voles and such every bit as much as red squirrels. Like fisher, marten often prefer mast from late summer on. Indeed I have seen where martens have given robins and evening grosbeaks quite a run for their money in attempting to hoard all the scarlet mountain ash berries when this ripening fruit lights up hilltops in the Great South Woods beginning in October.

Will the marten emulate the fisher by continuing its reoccupation of the entire Adirondack Park and eventually extend to the St. Lawrence Valley and other low-lying areas? The marten is more dependent on mature forest than the fisher, but in light of the marten's graphic range extension in the past two decades it might be unwise to dismiss the possibility. Stay tuned!

OTTER

This striking predator is the third member of the mustelid tribe that achieves near-maximum numbers in population in the Great South Woods and the Adirondacks generally. The otter exhibits a difference, though, both in the aquatic lifestyle it revels in and in the fact that it is the largest member of the clan present unless the wolverine has managed to stay hidden in some secluded nook in the forest. Unlike the others, otter numbers appear to stay fairly stable year after year.

Over the years I have witnessed a varied repertory of otter antics, both visual and vocal. I have heard them uttering various perplexing "eek" sounds as they shot their reptilian heads in and out of the water. Shades of Loch Ness and Champ! I've also often heard a hoarse grunt as they simultaneously swam near and raised their heads to get a better view of the object of their curiosity (me). On two rather puzzling occasions I've been privy to a medley of growls, screams, and hisses as a group of otters apparently waged fratricidal warfare among each other! There was violence, but it was decidedly mitigated and held on a leash. I ponder the reason for this activity to this very day. A sense of frustration emerges, but also a feeling of awareness that there remains so much in the forest that eludes our comprehension.

Otter dens are always near water, often in abandoned beaver lodges. They also den in banks and in hollow forest giants that are slumbering away, in prone positions near sources of permanent water.

In winter, otters seem to get a sense of wanderlust for they take long slides through the snow. Often their paths go from one stream clear to another. The smooth trough made by the otter is often used by other creatures in winter. I often note bobcats, gray fox, and red fox using these highways over the snow.

On several occasions on the Bog River and once on the South Branch of the Grass River, I came upon otter feeding on mussels or crayfish on large boulders while I was paddling a bend in the river. The otter reached the water so fast I was unable to decide if they slid or jumped!

Mussels are frequently eaten by otters and their shells discarded after the feast. This is a frequent sight along rivers in the region. The shells, singly or in small piles, are frequently on boulders or up on banks. Larger piles are from muskrat and I see them most often under cover since the muskrat is not as impervious to an aerial attack from a large raptor as is the otter.

The otter is a vital link between the waters and the woods and its absence would be akin to removing a solid length of chain in the circular ecosystem that makes up the Great South Woods!

RAPTORS

Swiftly, surely and lethally they fly by day and night, bringing woe to a legion of other creatures. They are the avian raptors and they perform a similar function in an ecosystem to that of mammal predators, whose role they often complement. The Great South Woods is blessed with a varied assemblage of these avian predators, including a few quite rare today in the rest of the Northeast.

Owls are the rulers of the Adirondack skies with the advent of darkness upon the landscape. The Great South Woods hosts a number of these nocturnal predators as breeding species, while another group of owls often descends upon the area with the coming of winter.

One starry summer night I came upon an entrancing and puzzling sight as I was driving on State Highway 3 adjacent to Peavine Swamp in the town of Clifton. A porcupine with its legs broken and a patch of skin removed from its dorsal section lay slumped on the highway. Nearby, floundering helplessly on the roadway, was a barred owl. I alighted from the vehicle and prodded the porcupine with a beaver stick I had handy. After an interval the owl finally flew awkwardly off into the darkness. The porcupine was beyond help and had to be put down to relieve its suffering.

After a slight reflection I was able to piece together what had occurred. The porcupine had been struck by a vehicle and incapacitated. The owl came upon this scene and promptly attacked the hapless porcupine. The owl did not count on a few of the porcupine's quills being able to temporarily impair its power of flight. So it was until my entrance upon the scene. A sight never to be forgotten!

Barred owls make use of old snags standing in the forest for most of their nest sites. I often hear them calling during the hours of daylight, especially when conditions are cloudy.

That "tiger of the deep woods," the great horned owl, is less common in the Great South Woods than the barred. Despite their nickname, in our region their base is mainly on the periphery of the area and in large, open tracts. I often find them reusing the nest of a hawk in constructing their natal rearing place.

The great horned definitely take larger prey than the barred as a rule. Striped skunks and house cats are a regular part of their prey base, although in the Great South Woods the latter are more likely to be picked off by coyotes. This is especially so in the vicinity of the hamlets.

For years a perplexing situation occurred with enough regularity to vex as well as mystify me. This was the case of the "headless hares." On a number of occasions I came across the corpses of snowshoe hares lying on the forest floor totally intact except for one significant fact. They were minus their heads! The mystery was solved when I saw a great horned owl fly away from one of the hapless hares.

Saw-whet owls also breed on a regular basis in the Great South Woods. I often hear their monotonous, metallic "toot" sound coming from the depths of white cedar swamps from March through May, when breeding males are courting females. These little owls apparently fly low, for on two occasions I have come upon their bodies lying lifeless on highways after being struck by vehicles.

The winter season sees a southward migration to our area of owls that breed in the far north. Indeed, the Great South Woods and its environs are among the best places south of the Canadian border to see these glorious raptors. And see them one may, for these northern owls are diurnal as well as nocturnal.

The great gray owl leads the pack locally. Every few years numbers of them put in an appearance. The hawk owl and boreal owl are also occasionally seen. So, too, the wondrous white snowy owl, although it is more commonly seen in the St. Lawrence Valley where the open farmlands more nearly resemble the familiar tundra it left back home.

In addition to the cryptic golden eagle, two other species of eagle reside in the Great South Woods. Bald eagles seem to be slowly on the increase after being restored to the Adirondacks by the DEC. Several pairs are now breeding locally with production of young varying from year to year.

They have recently begun to appear locally in winter. Numbers have varied from three to eight individuals and they appear to be sustained almost exclusively by the nutrients contained in the carcasses of wintering white-tailed deer. Thus they have built up quite an intricate relationship with fellow scavengers such as ravens and coyotes. They both complement and compete with the ravens and coyotes for the vital sustenance that these carcasses provide. Without these carcasses there would be no eagles present during the season of snow.

The fish-eagle or osprey is also a fairly common local nester. The nests are almost invariably located on huge white pines adjacent to large bodies of water. I'm always on the lookout to report such nest sites to the DEC as the local regional office monitors them closely.

I've been thrilled on a number of occasions by the sight of an osprey plunging into the water to secure a fish for consumption. I sharply recall two instances, in particular, at one of the tiny five ponds which collectively have given us the name "Five Ponds Wilderness Area." I have never, however, been rewarded by the sight of a bald eagle diving at the osprey and forcing it to relinquish its hard-earned prey!

Goshawks, these great glorious gray raptors of the north woods, also find congenial habitat in our Great South Woods. The nests of this species I have seen have been in large beech trees, which makes me ponder their future as local trees continue to succumb to beech disease.

The goshawks are quite aggressive around the nest site in defense of their young. I remember an especially bellicose pair that dive-bombed me with such ardor in the Cranberry Lake Wild Forest that I felt fortunate to withdraw from the area with my hide still intact!

Some goshawks will also winter in the Great South Woods. I see them around deer feeding stations where they lie in wait for the wintering song birds that also avail themselves of the cracked corn put out for the deer.

At these winter sites they are joined by another of the "blue darter" tribe, the sharp-shinned hawk. The sharp-shinned is the ultimate destroyer of birds in the vicinity of a winter feeder. In fact I am certain that it spends the winter in the Great South Woods only for the bounteous larder provided by these feeding stations.

The sharp-shinned is considerably smaller than the goshawk and not often seen in summer. Usually it flies low and restricts its flight to the interior of the woods. Because of this furtiveness it is not often seen, but I have occasionally spied them in the deep woods near Dead Creek Flow in the Five Ponds Wilderness.

The final "blue darter" is the Coopers hawk. Midway in size between the above two, it is more frequently seen than the sharp-shinned. I do not believe it is as common a breeder as the latter, although I have come upon nest sites on two occasions. At one site on the Beaver River a pair of Coopers was almost as belligerent toward a passing paddler as the goshawk normally is!

Falcons also have a presence in the Great South Woods and that presence seems to be increasing. Peregrine falcons, like the bald eagle, were also restored to the Adirondacks by a hacking program. Most nesting sites are on ledges in the eastern Adirondacks. That situation could be changing however, as peregrines have been observed, in summer, in the vicinity of Lows Lake and in several of the interior mountain areas where they formerly had eyries.

Another falcon, the merlin, provides the classic example of a cryptic creature that has recently "emerged from the shadows." Although it was previously not known to breed south of the Canadian border, I often see it in the summertime in the Great South Woods. Given my proclivity toward these "creatures of the shadow," I had often wondered about the possibility of local breeding and mentioned such to a prominent state ornithologist around 1980. After all, no less a personage than Teddy Roosevelt had raised the possibility of merlin breeding in the Adirondacks over a century ago!

These musings came to fruition in the 1990s when merlin were reported breeding near the St. Regis Lakes and also in the vicinity of

Lake Placid. Several more have been chronicled since then, including one by the sprawling Massawepie Peatland complex. The case of the merlin buoys optimism that other creatures of the shadow will have their day of re-emergence!

The kestrel is the third and most common of the falcons. Open areas with adjacent hollow trees are its habitat requirement. Since these open areas are not as common in the Great South Woods as in the St. Lawrence Valley, neither is the kestrel. There may have been a slight decline in numbers recently in both areas.

The buteos are probably the most common group of three hawk species that breed in the Great South Woods. A fourth is a common winter visitor from the far north.

Breeding broad-winged hawks reach near their maximum possible numbers in the Adirondack Park. They come in May and are all gone in September, a brief sojourn. Their nests are usually in small openings in extensive woodlands. Most of the ones I have seen have been in the crotches of yellow birch trees.

I have watched broad-winged hawks swoop on a red-backed vole that was storing the fruits of black cherry one late August day. Its talons were fully extended, and away went the hawk accompanied by one hapless vole. I have seen them also, on a number of occasions, carry off small snakes and frogs.

Very recently I feel there has been a modest decline in the number of broad-winged hawks breeding locally. I attribute this mainly to an increase in the local population of two other buteos, the red-tailed and red-shouldered hawks.

The red-tailed hawk seems to have had a dramatic increase in its breeding population recently. At least this is what I have observed in my area of the Great South Woods. Large trees in the vicinity of extensive open areas seem to be essential for successful breeding. Large marshes and old beaver flows appear to fit the bill in the Great South Woods. Unlike in other areas of the state, nests are fairly commonly placed in conifer trees locally. I have seen them both in white pine and red spruce. Soaring pairs of this large raptor are truly impressive, especially since it is a sight I never thought I would see in the middle of the Five Ponds Wilderness!

The red-shouldered hawk has also increased in numbers locally during the breeding season. Active beaver flows rather than abandoned ones seem to be the habitat of preference. The one nest I was able to discover was in a yellow birch. Their calls are now much more in evidence than they were even a decade ago. Care has to be exercised here as blue jays often imitate the call of red-shouldered hawks, although with a little experience the actual hawk calls can always be discerned.

Rough-legged hawks, large buteos of the open tundra, often appear here in winter. As open farmland bears a nearer resemblance to tundra than does forest, they are more likely to be seen in the St. Lawrence Valley than in the Great South Woods. The top of Tug Hill also possesses an appeal for them.

An intriguing occurrence transpired on the abandoned farmlands of Fort Drum during the summer of 1994. A local ornithologist doing surveys there discovered that a pair of these hawks had remained through the summer. Although no nest was discovered, it did set my mind to thinking of possibilities in this direction.

It also set my mind to ponder on the dynamic nature of raptor populations and on what an integral parcel of the Great South Woods they most assuredly are. The forest bereft of its noble raptors would be impoverished every bit as much as it would be were its dramatic mammal predators missing!

II

OTHER WILDLIFE INHABITANTS

Photo courtesy of Betsy Tisdale

Snowshoe Hare

These are creatures that are far less dramatic in appearance than the ones discussed in the previous chapter. But many of them have an effect on the ecosystem that is every bit as dramatic as that produced by the more charismatic fauna.

They also have a tendency to interact more frequently with the human element in the Great South Woods. Many of them are among the species most frequently observed in interaction with humans in both a positive or negative fashion, depending on the species. They may provide the human observer with interest, joy, or irritation as the case may be, but above all they are an indispensable part of the fabric of the forest.

PREY

They are by most criteria not very glamorous, but in actuality they are the very firmament upon which much of the entire ecosystem is built. Without their presence there would not be enough sufficient nutrients available to support the ecosystem's predators and scavengers.

These are in fact the creatures that are both hunted by and sustain the dramatic predators of the Great South Woods. These prey species can also have a draconian effect on the area's vegetation. They in many respects determine what grows where and when. Uncontrolled by predators, they can eliminate certain species of flora from large areas of the forest.

I have limited the prey species discussed here to mammals and one species of bird. It is wise to remember, however, that herptiles and insects also serve a role as prey species in certain cases. Some species (deer, beaver, wild turkey, cottontail, etc.) have been excluded because they have been discussed in detail elsewhere. The creatures that I speak of here are those that are not only the backbone of the ecosystem, but also those that most likely will be seen during a sojourn to the Great South Woods.

CHIPMUNK

These handsome little ground squirrels appear to be ubiquitous in the Great South Woods. They appear readily in a variety of situations, at least for seven months of the year. For the other approximately five months Adirondack chipmunks solve the problem of severe winter weather by resorting to a lengthy period of hibernation.

Chipmunks usually embark on an eating binge before entering this period of dormancy. The ridges of the Great South Woods are alive with chipmunks scampering to and fro in October in an earnest quest to devour as many beechnuts as they can before the long sleep sets in. I have on a number of occasions seen them high up in the branches of black cherry trees during this season, not wishing to wait for the cherries to fall before devouring them.

At this time and throughout the year chipmunks are quite vulnerable to predators. Their nemeses here are avian as well as mammalian. Hawks take a considerable toll on their numbers. I have seen both broad-winged and red-shouldered hawks attack chipmunks and carry them off. House cats are also quite lethal to chipmunks. In the vicinity of my house in the town of Fine these minute squirrels have been eliminated for a distance of 1,000 feet or more by the house cats that freely range from the residences of neighbors. Not exactly cricket, as house cats always have their cat chow to resort to in difficult times!

Chipmunks are fed often at various lean-tos located in the Great South Woods. Usually they are there waiting expectantly within ten minutes of one's setting up camp. Despite its cuteness and gaudiness the chipmunk does have a streak of violence that occasionally complements its normal vim and vigor. One of the more entrancing sights I have been rewarded with is that of an enraged chipmunk chasing a woodland jumping mouse into Glasby Pond. The jumping mouse escaped only by swimming across the pond. You never know!

After gorging on beechnuts, chipmunks retreat in October to the vicinity of their burrows, where they let forth a series of "cuck-cucks" that resonate throughout the autumn woods. Then they disappear to later present the sight of a joyous awakening to cabin-weary humans when they come forth from their slumber just as the emerging spring brings a renewal of life to the forest.

RED SQUIRREL

The red squirrel is equally abundant and almost as ubiquitous as the chipmunk in the Great South Woods. There are differences, however. The primary one is that the red squirrel graces the forest with its presence for the full duration of the year rather than half of it.

Squirrels survive the winter by feeding heavily on the seeds contained in conifer cones. Thus this type of forest is especially relished by red squirrels. Mature deciduous forests also harbor good populations. I have noticed that populations of red squirrels fluctuate wildly in our area. When numbers are depressed it sometimes appears that the only areas harboring them are conifer forests and mature tracts of broad-leafed trees.

Like chipmunks, red squirrels haunt certain lean-tos seeking a handout. Fungi are used heavily in autumn and early winter. The sight of fungi wedged into conifer trees during this period is one that never fails to start me musing on squirrels and mushrooms and such.

Red squirrels are, in many respects, as much ground dwellers as tree climbers. They often go underground, especially in winter. I often see the tracks of pursuing marten during this time. The marten go right down under the fallen logs and debris in pursuit of the red squirrel lying there. Mink pursue them in this fashion also. Many times the squirrels enter the snow to retrieve conifer cones they have buried in or on the ground. White pine and Norway spruce cones are particularly beloved, it seems.

This squirrel is the original whistle-blower of the Great South Woods. Long before even the blue jay, it will give its chattering call to alert all in hearing of the presence of a human or a predator. A clucking sound usually means a raptor is nearby. I once watched, enthralled, as a red squirrel clucked repeatedly while facing down a red-tailed hawk that sat not twenty feet from it in the top of an adjacent Scotch pine. The confused raptor eventually flew off into the forest.

Memories such as this are as cherished as those of seeing one of the "creatures of the shadow." The Great South Woods would not be the same without encounters like these and without the presence of this mundane little creature that makes sights such as this possible.

SNOWSHOE HARE

If there is one creature that shows the ideal adaptation to the Great South Woods, it is the snowshoe hare. It thrives on the habitat that is most common here: conifer woods, mature mixed forest with undergrowth, and alder swales. Its color is perfectly synchronized to its surroundings, from the brown in summer that matches the dappled forest understory to the ivory white of winter that merges into the snow-clad background present for five months of the year.

The snowshoe hare is pursued by practically all predators in the Great South Woods. I have often seen tracks denoting where even packs of large canids were pursuing it in the winter time of want. Even the larger of the two weasels present locally appears to pursue it as prey at this time of year. This is the long-tailed weasel; I have on a number of occasions witnessed its tracks following and deliberately searching out the hare in winter. Fisher and mink also follow its track at this time of year.

Hares feed on succulent greens during summer but do not seem to be a problem usually where home vegetable gardens are concerned. In twenty-three years I have had only minor annoyances from the hare as far as my garden is concerned. In winter I see hares feeding on the twigs of hardwoods and the needles of conifers. Blackberry and raspberry twigs are relished especially, as are the needles of balsam fir and spruce. The latter is in sharp contrast to deer who usually completely disdain an offering of spruce. During severe winters hares begin to consume the bark of hardwoods. Old apple trees and sumac are particularly favored.

Hares are generally not too much in evidence around the lean-tos of our region but I have on a number of occasions seen apparently tame hares on top of Algonquin Mountain being fed by hikers. I attribute this lack of fear to the fact that hares up this high are not hunted due to the difficulty of transporting them back to the trailhead.

Mad as a March hare! This nuptial exuberance manifested by thumping around a lean-to at night and darting erratically on and off highways is more accurately relegated to April in our territory. No matter, the Great South Woods would bemoan this loss of vernal zaniness as much as the local predators would suffer a lack of protein if the snowshoe hare were ever to disappear from the forest.

RUFFED GROUSE

Populations of ruffed grouse in the Great South Woods are notable for undergoing radical population swings. Unlike the hare whose population shifts occur on a regular cyclic basis (not as dramatic in the Adirondacks as farther north) the pulsating of grouse populations is solely induced by environmental factors. Thus these shifts in populations are irregular.

Wet, cold spring weather is devastating to young grouse. A warm summer of moderate rainfall can encourage insect numbers and help to partially offset this plunge in numbers.

Grouse switch to fruit and mast in late summer. In winter they are tantalized by the buds of apple trees, but it is the black cherry tree and its buds that are even more important, for the latter is a much more common tree in the Adirondack forest. The catkins of aspen attain prominence in the diet of the grouse as winter progresses into spring.

Grouse seek shelter under the snow in winter. As often as I see grouse "budding" black cherry in winter, I have also been startled by the explosion of a grouse rocketing airborne from its retreat under the insulation of the snow pack. Conifer cover is important at this time of year also. It furnishes warmth and protection from predators in this stressful season.

A host of avian and mammalian predators include the grouse as a regular tidbit on their menu. The goshawk, gray ghost of the forest, strives in all seasons to do its utmost to decimate grouse numbers. I was fortunate enough to witness one kill of a grouse by a goshawk and it is a sight I will long remember. It was difficult to observe but quite dramatic and definitely apart of the natural order.

Almost every red fox den that I've found had grouse feathers present at some time during the year. These and the feet of rabbits seem always to adorn the mound in front of the den.

Try as I may I'm unable to envision the forest of the Great South Woods without the ruffed grouse rocketing in flight through it as it flees, with all its might, from one of its predators.

PORCUPINE

This walking pincushion is another specialty of the boreal forest. Porcupines grow quite large upon occasion; I have seen a number of whoppers in my travel.

The lethal-looking quills that adorn this large rodent all over, except on the undersides, afford it a good deal of protection. Most predators are precluded from including porcupines in their diet because of this armament. Cats often breach this armor, however, and the indefatigable fisher merely finds it a minor annoyance as it proceeds on its rounds of regularly feasting on the flesh of porcupine.

Fisher, in fact, meticulously seek out porcupine in winter. There has been much conjecture as to exactly how fisher are able to dispatch porcupine without incurring the wrath of their quills. In two cases I have seen the fisher overcome the porcupine's defense by repeated, lightning-like thrusts to the head area. In one case the fisher ascended a tree to attack the porcupine.

Bobcats also prey fairly successfully on porcupine, especially in winter. There is some evidence that they may flip the "porky" over on its dorsal area and attack the unprotected underparts. In winter I often note signs of both fisher and bobcat following the tracks of porcupine.

Succulent vegetation is the porcupine's preferred bill of fare during summer. This includes water plants, which accounts for their propensity for swimming. A craving for sodium is also characteristic; this may be satisfied by a water lily as well as a block of salt. Tender young leaves of deciduous trees also suffice in supplying this succulent vegetation. Basswood trees seem especially beloved to porcupine, who may often be seen high up on their upper branches munching away.

In winter the needles of conifers and the tender bark of young saplings are the leading items on the menu. Hemlock needles are particularly cherished and the ground beneath them is littered with boughs cut by porcupine at this time of year. Deer and snowshoe hare avail themselves almost instantly of this unexpected bounty. The bark of young yellow birch, beech, red maple, balsam fir, and white pine is attacked with gusto during this season, especially in the vicinity of the rock fissures that often are the denning sites in winter. This girdling often kills the young trees and acts as a decided pruning agent in thinning out the forest. Indeed, barren would be the Great South Woods without the quill pig!

CREATURES of the EDGE

Here we come to the creatures that are on the absolute fringe of their range in the Great South Woods. For them the habitat locally ranges from minimal to marginal. Many are, in addition, on the periphery of their continental range. The marginality of habitat springs mainly from the severity of winter weather in the Great South Woods. This is the universal limiting factor, either directly or indirectly.

Populations vary quite dramatically from year to year. Wildly fluc-
tuating weather patterns account for this. The creatures appear and vanish often in response to the variations in weather. From my general
observations in the Adirondack Park over the last three decades, this
appears to be their lot at large here. Stable populations are normally
present only on the perimeter of the Big Woods or in the vicinity of
hamlets. Still, the dash of diversity they provide is quite welcome!

COTTONTAIL

The original Peter Rabbit and the bunny of the briar patch in the
tales of Uncle Remus, the cottontail is the rabbit of substance over
most of the Northeast. In the Great South Woods, however, it is relegated to a relatively minor role. This apparently exists as a direct result
of the heavy snow cover during even an average winter here. The depth
of snow precludes any possibility of the cottontail being able to move
easily at this time of year. It simply has not evolved to be as compatible
with snow as has the snowshoe hare!

For most of the year there is ample food available in the Great
South Woods for this rabbit although I'm sure it bemoans the scarcity
of vegetable gardens. Unlike the hare, the cottontail has a positive penchant to demolish as much of a garden as it can.

In the Adirondack Park the cottontail is most often restricted to the
park's periphery as well as the vicinity of hamlets. After mild winters
they spread out into the surrounding terrain, where they proliferate for
a few years until being decimated by the next harsh winter. At least this
has been my experience gleaned from a quarter century of observation.

There is another limiting factor; the vulnerability of cottontails to
predators during winter. Its brown fur contrasted with the background
of white proves a magnet for every hungry carnivore. Human predators
not known for sportsmanship also harvest them at this time of year.

Indian Creek Nature Center and the surrounding Upper and Lower
Lakes Wildlife Management Area near Canton seem to be the line of
demarcation between hares and cottontails. In general, cottontails become more abundant than hares north of there until they become dominant in the vicinity of the St. Lawrence River. Hunting tallies at the
Wildlife Management Area are often split almost in half between the

two species. How long a situation like this can prevail is uncertain. It may take a century or more to resolve where one species finally replaces the other.

Personally, I'll share my vegetable patch with such a fetching creature without so much as a second thought!

GRAY SQUIRREL

Gray squirrels take a definite back seat in the Great South Woods to the ever-present red squirrel. Like the cottontail, they are common enough in the St. Lawrence Valley, but are generally restricted to hamlets and the periphery of the big woods.

There are a number of reasons for this, but primarily it's the severity of winter weather as is the case for the cottontail. With the gray squirrel, however, the main limiting factor appears to be snow depth rather than cold. I have seen gray squirrels cavorting in the trees in sub-zero weather when nary a red squirrel could be seen outside its den.

The simple fact is that gray squirrels have not learned to utilize the abundant cones of conifers that exist in the winter landscape of the Great South Woods and that do much toward sustaining the red squirrel in this season of want. The gray is restricted to foraging in areas of light snow cover where it can retrieve the nuts of oak and beech that lie buried under the snow. The scarcity of oak locally does not help matters either.

Feeding on sunflower seeds around hamlets has enabled gray squirrels to achieve restricted populations in their vicinities. From here they colonize adjoining areas with beech and oak especially. With a guaranteed severe Adirondack winter every few years, it all comes to naught as they perish completely in these outlying areas.

Legend proclaims that the red squirrel is dominant over the gray squirrel and maintains this mastery by aggressive assaults on the gray. I have witnessed attacks by reds on grays on two separate occasions, so there is no doubt they occur. Still I am withholding judgment on the theory of absolute mastery. In fact in a few hamlets, Wanakena for one, an increase in population of gray squirrels heralded a decided decrease in the population of red!

The grays have a definite penchant for summer wandering in response to population pressures. Locally this is not as pronounced as it is downstate. I have seen limited examples of the road carnage that ensues from this wanderlust on two occasions in the St. Lawrence Valley. Never really in the Great South Woods, however.

I admit to being somewhat enamored of the gray squirrel and to having done much in the way of winter feeding to encourage its presence around my residence. It recalls pleasant memories of a past era, but in addition I feel it adds a bit to both the sparkle and the biodiversity of the Great South Woods.

WILD TURKEY

There is an ongoing and at times lively debate locally as to whether wild turkeys were indigenous to the Great South Woods before the advent of European colonization. Each side of this debate has its staunch advocates, unable to agree on this central issue. They do agree, however, that the wild turkey is now fairly well established throughout the Great South Woods.

This came about primarily from the introduction of wild-trapped individuals at Fort Drum and in the St. Lawrence Valley. From there they spread slowly to the Great South Woods. Today they are scattered throughout the Big Woods with the main impediment to their proliferation being the severity of winter weather.

Once again the snow depth, rather than the cold, appears to be the main culprit. Turkeys find it extremely difficult to scratch through an extensive and deep snow cover to obtain food. They frequent the vicinity of springs and rivulets, where the bare ground often is at or near the surface. Insect eggs, larvae, all sorts of greens and other goodies are there for the taking.

For the same reason, wild turkeys go from one deer bed to another under the conifers in winter. I often follow their tracks and find where the body of a reclining deer has melted the snow and revealed the bare ground or nearly so. Here I watch them scratch away at the ground in apparent bliss while I ponder on the reality of a wild creature's adaptation to its habitat.

Wild turkeys also feed on the buds of red maple in winter, littering the ground with such a profusion of twigs that it seems that someone has taken a hatchet to the branches of the trees.

Turkeys also relish newly-spread manure placed on fields. These often contain edible seeds, as well as insects, to their delight. The few dairy operations remaining in the town of Pitcairn and the sole beef operation in the town of Fine help, I feel, to bolster local populations. So do the winter deer feeding stations where I have counted as many as eighteen turkeys at one feeding. This does not compare to the flocks of thirty to forty individuals I have seen in late summer when several hens combine their broods for security when feeding. A sentinel is always placed here to watch out for threats to the flock. In winter, however, I have not noticed this safety measure being taken.

Friends relayed an incident to me wherein a wild turkey was allegedly killed by an immature bald eagle in December 1995. I arrived at the scene shortly after the occurrence and concluded that this was in fact what had happened, although, considering the circumstance, I feel the "perpetrator" was more apt to be a golden eagle, which dispatches prey much more readily at this time of year than does the more carrion-feeding bald eagle.

Regarding eagles and turkeys, Benjamin Franklin once proposed the wild turkey as the symbol of our country. In this, of course, it would have replaced the bald eagle. I'm not prepared to go that far, but it sure is pleasant having the wild turkey in our Great South Woods.

GRAY FOX

A blur of grizzled silver passed in the gloaming of an October twilight as it crossed Route 3 in the town of Pitcairn just ahead of my vehicle. So rapid was its motion that it reminded me of nothing less than a silver bullet.

To date this has been the only gray fox my eyes have actually laid sight on in the Great South Woods. This is not to say they aren't around, at least sparingly. Two trapper acquaintances of mine have taken five between them in the past twenty years. I usually see their winter tracks in the snow at least once each season. Their tracks are quite distinctive, midway in size and roundness between a red fox and a house cat. They seem quite ill at ease in deep snow so it is obvious that this is the prime limiting factor locally. I once followed a gray fox track for over half a mile as it meticulously walked in the smooth glazed path of an otter sliding through the snow!

To a certain extent, gray fox also possess the un-canine trait of being able to climb trees. This feline trait has helped to earn it the title of "cat fox" which seasoned woodsmen often bestow. They utilize this climbing ability mainly to escape larger predators. However, on at least one occasion, I have seen evidence denoting where a gray fox ascended twelve feet up a chokecherry for the puckerish fruit festooning its upper branches so liberally.

Unlike red fox, gray fox most often use rocky fissures and small caverns as den sites. The two fox types are thus able to coexist in harmony. They do so, in fact, fairly frequently in the southern Adirondacks. Perhaps some day soon this will be the situation in the Great South Woods also!

OPOSSUM

This was an animal whose presence was whispered about in the "Big Woods" of old Flushing, Long Island. Some swore it was there, but others steadfastly denied it. Anyhow, the habitat left available was fading fast as urban development proceeded apace. This is somewhat similar to the situation prevailing in the Great South Woods today, although the marginality in habitat results from, as usual, the severity of winter weather .

The presence of the opossum locally is attested to by sporadic road kills. The irregularity of these kills denotes that the opossum, like other "creatures of the edge" here, waxes and wanes in population depending on weather.

I have seen opossum in garages on two occasions, proving that the hamlets have an attraction for them also. This is especially so in winter. One time, in the hamlet of Fine, one was sharing a bowl of milk with a half-grown house cat.

The opossum has very sparse fur for winter protection and, in addition, has not developed the art of hibernation for survival during this time of harshness and want. As a result it must forage abroad all winter for nourishment. In doing so it is much more vulnerable to attack from the elements than are other winter foragers. I recall quite vividly an encounter I had with a roadside opossum in the town of Clare a decade ago. The forlorn creature was the picture of perfect misery, wandering in an aimless fashion with the tips of its ears completely frozen off!

In spite of all the above, the opossum goes plodding on, apparently nonplussed by all the hostile aspects of climate and terrain allied against it. An eating and breeding machine of a primitive order, it is perhaps too dim-witted to perceive the reality of adversity. So it marches forward into the twenty-first century.

WINGED HORRORS

So lethal a mite that it may move a mountain: perhaps there is no description more apt than this when referring to the various biting insects that plague the Great South Woods at certain times of the year. They were probably at least partially responsible for the delayed settlement of the region and even today discourage hordes of visitors that might otherwise descend on the area. Indeed, proponents of tourism in the region regularly bemoan the fact that the prevalence of these noxious insects contrives to render one whole month of the year null and void as far as tourism is concerned. That month is June when the pestilence of these insects is absolutely at its zenith.

Some resort owners have, in the past, been in favor of aerial spraying to neutralize the effects of these insect pests on the citizenry. BT, which is target-specific by attacking the larvae of only a few related insect forms, has been accepted by many as a compromise. This relatively innocuous bacteria causes far less damage to the environment than the random spraying of chemicals from the air. The controversy even extended to insecticides that are put on the individual directly to dissuade the noxious horde. DEET, one of the most effective in this regard, has been banned and unbanned depending on who is currently occupying the Governor's mansion!

The chronology of unpleasantry commences with the emergence of adult blackflies in mid-May. They are usually out a week before commencing to bite, but when they begin they become an absolute horror for the remainder of the spring. They have a penchant to swarm in the eyes and ears of hapless victims as well as delivering a bite. While they are in the process of belaboring me during this season, I take solace in the fact they are generally gone by July and also do not bite in the evening or inside houses. I am also mollified somewhat by the thought that they must have cool, clear, unpolluted running water to breed in. So an appearance by them might mean paradoxically that something is right with the environment!

Mosquitoes are next to arrive on the scene. They do bite at night and inside houses and tents and, in addition, have the longest flying (and biting) period of any of the insects described. They attain a little redemption in my eyes by being smaller and less bothersome than the mosquitoes of the St. Lawrence Valley.

The deerfly comes on the scene in the high noon of summer. It waxes (and bites) prolifically on days of bright sunshine. Its piercing bite is the worst single attack of all. Certain people, myself included, may acquire a slight allergic reaction from its attention. I usually suffer in silence and wait for darkness to descend. Horseflies, called more appropriately mooseflies by some locals, are related to deerflies and also possess a very painful bite.

Punkies, also referred to as "no-see-ums," are quite sporadic in their appearance in the Great South Woods. I encounter them only a few times every year, usually on extremely humid evenings. Their forte in misery is the fact they are so tiny that they can penetrate through the smallest screens to wreak havoc on the inhabitants inside.

Come late August and the litany of horrors has run its course for the year. For three months it has probably dissuaded vast numbers of the populace from descending on the Big Woods. This fact alone enables me to tolerate the torture that is handed out so lavishly to all!

HERPTILES

This is the collective name that scientists have recently bestowed on amphibians and reptiles. Since the early 1990s, New York State has conducted an annual survey to determine which members of this zoological category reside in the state. I am one of the relatively few recorders in southern St. Lawrence County and have participated in the survey from its onset. In the course of my participation I have run into some interesting tidbits indeed.

To begin with, the Great South Woods is not the proverbial cup of joy for most herptiles. These cold-blooded creatures require warmth and heat in abundance since their body temperatures are regulated by the surrounding weather. As any veteran woodsmen hereabouts can relate, this is not a commodity in bounteous supply in the Great South Woods or in the Adirondacks in general.

Only the most hardy of herptiles can survive here and to do so they must improvise dramatically. They do this by undergoing a winter hibernation period of from six to nine months to overcome the vicissitudes of winter.

Many are unable to do this. Some of the most common herptiles in the rest of the state are missing locally. Those that do overcome these hardships are often abundant and even adapt to new niches in the Great South Woods. This is probably a little bit of evolution in action right before our eyes!

Another interesting facet regarding their presence is a seeming paradox of dispersal and occurrence. The herptiles most common in the Great South Woods are quite often the ones most common in the urban parks of our largest cities, including Central Park in New York City. Indeed, in the latter areas they are usually the only ones present. The common snapping turtle and the garter snake spring readily to mind. Apparently they can cope quite nicely with the rigors inherent in both urban life and the wilderness!

What accounts for this seeming mismatch of domiciles? I believe that it emanates from the simple, unassailable fact that Central Park and the Great South Woods are the extremes of inhospitality in the state as far as herptiles are concerned. They must overcome the lengthy winter in the one and human depredation in the other. Only the hardiest can do this, the survival of the fittest if you will!

The turtles are few in number with only one, the snapping turtle, truly abundant. The snapper is quite ubiquitous and liable to turn up just about anywhere in the Great South Woods. Some get to be truly huge—I've heard of them getting to thirty pounds locally and even larger elsewhere.

One fact of their existence posed a true mystery to me until I was enlightened by an old-time woodsman. For years I had observed where turtle eggs were continually being dug up and devoured seemingly as quickly as they could be laid by the female snappers. Coyotes, fox, 'coons, skunks—all seemed to participate in the bounty! How could viable populations be maintained in the face of such assaults upon the nest generation? "Simple," replied my pragmatic friend with the wisdom of the woods—"How long do snapping turtles live?" "Up to sixty years and more," I replied. "How many eggs are laid per year?" "A hundred or so," I replied! "Just think," said he, "that snapper need have only two of these thousands survive to maturity in order to replace her and her mate!" I often do think of that and also of the fact that not all wisdom lies in the classroom!

The attractive painted turtle is also fairly common locally. I spy them sunning themselves on warm days on top of muskrat and beaver lodges.

The only other turtle I have encountered in the Great South Woods is the rare wood turtle. I have come upon it four times in twenty years, always on land. Once it appeared to be feeding on the fruit of a raspberry which had fallen to the ground.

There are, likewise, but few species of snakes in the Big Woods. Most common by far is the garter snake, which lives in a variety of habitats. It seems to be more aquatic locally; I often see it swimming, usually in streams. One place where it is especially abundant is above High Falls on the Oswegatchie River. The snakes here appear much larger and darker than normal. They are called water snakes by local woodsmen, but true water snakes in our area are restricted to the St. Lawrence Valley and the eastern Adirondacks.

I often observe garter snakes preying on toads as the latter hop across woodland trails. The toad has acquired a venom that deters mammalian predators, but apparently not the garter snake.

Our local garter snakes are also more aggressive than ones I have encountered elsewhere. I don't believe I have ever handled one that did not attempt to bite!

I occasionally come across green snakes in grass swales and on the edges of peatlands. They are invariably gentle and I have never had one attempt to bite. The secretive red-bellied snake is sometimes discovered under logs or debris in the forest. Not often do I find these handsome creatures, perhaps once every couple of years. They are cryptic in nature, but still I believe they are uncommon in the Great South Woods.

The only other snake I have come across here is the milk snake. Called "copperhead" locally, it is abundant on an abandoned farm across the road from my house. I never fail to lift the cover off a derelict well on a bright sunny day without finding several of these striking reptiles curled together.

The amphibian chorus begins with the wood frog and the leopard frog putting in an appearance just before the famous spring peeper chorus is about to take off. I have even seen leopard frogs against a background of snow in early April. They are more common in the St. Lawrence Valley than the Great South Woods, however. The reverse situation exists with the pickerel frog, which is commonly seen hopping through grassy swales in search of insects in summer.

The mink frog is also a northern specialty. I hear its metallic calls from June on, often in association with bull and green frogs.

These three are usually the last of the chorus to serenade the forest. They call all through the hot, humid days of early summer. Some of the larger ponds produce bull frogs of an ample enough size to furnish the proverbial frog legs for Epicureans.

The American toad can be found continually plodding across hiking trails in summer, seeking insects for sustenance. On good days I note as many as several score every mile. Also on these trails are garter snakes seeking the toads.

Gray tree frogs give their distinctive trilling call on extra-humid days. As this often heralds an approaching storm, local woodsmen frequently refer to them as rain frogs. I have seen their color vary with their background from the gray of tree bark to the yellow of goldenrod!

Salamanders, like frogs, are more successful in the Great South Woods than reptiles generally are. Still, they also can find the situation difficult at times. The most common species locally is the red-backed salamander. Shy and nocturnal by nature, it is not often encountered unless it is specifically searched for. Turning over enough downed logs and flattish stones will usually result in a sighting. Woodlands, especially more mature ones, are its preferred domain.

The gorgeously attired spotted salamander, like the wood frog, depends on the existence of temporary ponds for its breeding and egg-laying needs. These ponds, which owe their vernal existence entirely to snowmelt, are especially susceptible to acid rain. While populations may have been impacted to some degree, I still find the spotted to be ever present. This is another amphibian that has to be deliberately searched for to achieve any measure of success in locating it. Still, in winter they have come into my basement on several occasions.

The dusky salamander is occasionally seen near the banks of streams in our area. They are, however, nowhere near as common as I found them to be on Tug Hill.

The scarcity of the newt or "red eft," its land form, in the Great South Woods is somewhat perplexing. I've seen them on only three occasions in a quarter of a century, the last being ten years ago. One of the memories most treasured from Tug Hill is the spectacle of dozens of scarlet-skinned efts plodding across the forest floor after a spring or summer rain. I see the eft frequently today while hiking in the eastern Adirondacks, but not in the Great South Woods, which seems deprived of its presence. One conjecture has it that precipitation combined with the naturally acidic soils account for its absence. Whatever, I miss them and envy areas that still have them.

Participating in the state herptile survey has opened my eyes to how unique herptiles truly are in the Great South Woods. While the diversity is not great, their very presence here and the adaptations they have to undergo for survival is truly outstanding. The traits acquired here may, in fact, lead to new forms and even species somewhere down the line!

III

CREATURES OF THE SHADOW

Photo by Gerry Lemmo

Mountain Lion

We come now to animals of rumored existence—creatures purport-edly seen by many, but whose presence is generally steadfastly denied by officialdom. When they do acknowledge a specific encounter they are quick to consign it to the category of a meaningless escapee or re-leased individual.

The animals in question are part of the charismatic megafauna that allegedly expired completely around the turn of the century in the

Great South Woods. Like fireflies in the deep dusk, they roam in and out of the consciousness of Adirondackers today. They never quite go away, but are usually not dwelt on at any great length. Experienced woods people whisper of their existence. When they are surrounded by kindred spirits the whispers suddenly rise to a higher decibel.

What accounts for these continued, uninterrupted rumors and reports if there is no validity to them? If they are valid, why the difficulty in confirming their presence over the decades? It has recently been proposed that lovers of the Adirondack wilds have a deep inner need to believe in the existence of these spectacular wildlife species. I do not subscribe to this theory in the least! Adirondackers know full well what they are seeing in the vast majority of instances. The true situation regarding these "undocumented" species is quite complex and varies with the individual species being considered. In some cases there are formidable barriers against documenting their existence. Even if confirmed, the question arises, from whence did they come? This will be readily seen in a listing of the actual species.

I list them roughly according to the approximate number of sightings reported. The accounts include personal experiences with the animals in question as well as what I feel is their actual status in the Great South Woods as we enter the twenty-first century.

"Creatures of the shadow" they may be, but as may be seen from the individual accounts, some definitely are not yet in the twilight of their existence locally. Their continued presence enlivens the Great South Woods and lends that certain touch of splendor and mystique that makes it the premier wilderness in the East.

TIMBER WOLF

A long, low, tremulous howl came forth from somewhere on the mountain just as dusk descended. Haunting to a degree that sent a pleasant shudder to my spine, it was like no coyote call that I had ever heard. The sense of wonder it instilled was supplemented by the kindling of a spark of questioning deep in my psyche. If not a coyote, then what? The year was 1979 and the mountain was part of the Seward Range.

The last timber wolf allegedly verified in the Adirondacks was reported in 1899. That was the year that the final bounty payment was recorded for the carcass of a wolf. George Muir of the town of Fine, who was also instrumental in the demise of the cougar, was the person to whom the last bounty was paid. George, from all accounts, loved these splendid creatures in his own fashion and probably never dreamed that they could be driven to the brink of extirpation locally. They were however—the timber wolf was undoubtedly eliminated from the Adirondacks entirely, at least for a period of time. In this the wolf differs from the cougar, which I feel was never quite entirely eliminated from the Great South Woods.

The question arises: what of the situation today? We know there was a plethora of reports and confirmed kills of large canids coming in from the northwestern Adirondacks beginning around 1930. Some of these unusually large specimens were obviously hybrids, for this was the period when the coyote invaded the Adirondacks from Canada. The lack of mates initially resulted in numerous unions, often of coyotes and large domestic dogs. These unions occasionally resulted in the appearance of large wolf-like creatures to confuse the issue. They began to disappear in the 1950s as the coyote population stabilized and coyotes found no further need to mate with domestic canines.

Currently there are established populations of wolves as near to the Adirondacks as the Madawaska Highlands in Ontario and Laurentian Provincial Park in Quebec. In addition, the wolf is listed as a regular wanderer to Upper Canada Village Wildlife Refuge, just north of the border with New York State.

Do these wolves cross the Canadian border at times? Residents on the New York side of the St. Lawrence River have claimed for quite a while that they do. That fact was even acknowledged in a survey done as a master's thesis in conjunction with the effect of winter navigation on the St. Lawrence and wildlife populations. In addition, a biologist currently with the DEC has advised me that while formerly employed as a biologist for the U.S. Fish and Wildlife Service on Governor's Island in the St. Lawrence River, he twice witnessed what he claimed were timber wolves crossing the ice in winter. As he previously had been employed by the U.S. Fish and Wildlife as a biologist in Alaska, it is presumed he is aware of the difference between a wolf and a coyote! In addition to coming across the ice in winter, the wolf can enter New

York year-round via the sparsely populated land border with Quebec.

I have on a number of occasions come across tracks too large for any coyote, Eastern or otherwise, far back in the Forest Preserve during the middle of winter. I saw one on the ice at Buck Pond, eight miles through the forest from the nearest road of any sort, in the middle of the Five Ponds Wilderness where it definitely belongs.

Since that time when I was enchanted at the foot of the Seward Range, I have heard a similar rendition at infrequent intervals down through the years. More often that not, this stentorian howl was answered by a chorus of coyote howls off in the distance. Whether they're communicating or trying to intimidate with the force of numbers, I admit to being unsure of. Others have remarked on the same phenomenon. Friends who live in the isolated hamlet of Aldrich state that this is a regular occurrence.

I have also been made aware recently of a number of incidents that seem to buttress the case for the presence of at least the proverbial "lone wolf" in the Great South Woods during the past decade. This seems quite plausible, as solitary individuals spreading out from an established pack would herald the advent of any wolf colonization into a new area.

During the 1970s a wolf was killed by a vehicle near Caroga Lake in the southern Adirondacks. This was duly reported in *The Conservationist,* the official DEC magazine, in an issue shortly thereafter. The report was replete with pictures and described the "first wolf this century." It was then apparently consigned to the category of "never happened" and inquiries concerning the canid were met with the stock reply that it was presumed to be an escapee.

Then there was the seventy-three-pound canid killed by a bow hunter in the town of Hopkinton in the northern Adirondacks in the mid-1980s. Upon taking the pelt to a fur buyer in DeKalb Junction, he was informed that the creature in question was a wolf and was advised to discard it immediately. This he promptly did by burying the entire carcass. I was informed by the local DEC biologists that, out of curiosity, they prevailed upon him to show them where it was buried. They then sent the skull to the Smithsonian Institution in Washington, D.C., where the results confirmed that the skull was definitely that of a wolf—*canis lupus*. Knowing of my avid interest in this subject, the biologists informed me of what had transpired. They further added that a well-known local academician, who was an expert in the classifying of canids according to their cranial measurements, had also stated that based on the dimensions of the cranium he had no hesitation in classifying it as the Algonquin variety of wolf—*canis lupus lycaon.* This he confirmed to me when I made a follow-up call. The variety of wolf in question could be significant because the Algonquin strain is the type found directly across the border from New York in Canada. Interestingly enough, when I encountered the mammalogist at a meeting about three months later at which the DEC management personnel were present and broached the subject with him, he claimed his initial identification was in error and that the creature in question was actually a wolf-dog hybrid. The plot thickens!

The Algonquin variety of wolf (a "type," not a sub-species) is unusually small for a wolf, with adult males weighing from fifty-five to eighty pounds. There is a fair amount of overlap here with large Eastern coyotes. In addition, the Algonquin wolf is also suffused with a reddish coloration throughout its pelt, as is the case with the Eastern coyote. This is completely unlike the large northern wolves, which generally are the ones shown on the screen or pictured in publications. It, therefore, comes as no surprise that I was a bit dubious concerning the seventy-one-pound specimen of a canid that I observed hanging in an outbuilding of the Dart Lake YMCA Camp near Big Moose. The animal, liberally sprinkled with red throughout, had been taken by the camp's caretaker, a former DEC employee. With the knowledge I now have, I believe I can dispel most of my reservations and attest that the animal in question was probably truly a wolf.

While on the subject of past history, I recall the alleged shooting of two "wolves" by Andrew Shuler during his reign at Streeter Lake. Local lore claims the two canids were in reality shot by his caretaker, Carlos Law. When an opportunity presented itself to visit the Adirondack Room in the Andrew Shuler building on the campus of Clarkson University in Potsdam, I eagerly accepted it. There, behind a glass case, were two specimens of what definitely appeared to be immature timber wolves. Thus they were identified by Shuler at the time of their demise, and such I believe them to be.

From the above accounts and others I believe that the wolf is present in the Great South Woods. They disperse across the St. Lawrence and into this area, apparently on at least a semi-regular basis. Of this I have no doubt. What happens after their arrival is not so certain. Demographic factors alone consign isolated individuals of a dispersing population to a precarious existence. Then, too, there is the possibility of hybridization with the large Eastern coyote and introgression of their genes into this population. This has probably occurred to a slight degree already in Canada with the Algonquin wolf. It is a known fact that red wolves, timber wolves, coyotes, and feral dogs will freely interbreed with each other when there is a shortage of suitable mates in their own population. It is distinctly possible, therefore, that in order to produce a viable population with self-contained packs the wolf will need the aid of its former persecutor, Homo sapiens.

This situation has been somewhat befuddled lately by statements attributed to at least one source in the DEC pronouncing the wolf never inhabited New York State. I find this quite perplexing, unless nineteenth-century canids were literate and able to decipher signs on the borders of New York and adjacent states and provinces to the effect that they should stay out. I truly hope this is not just a political ploy to prevent man, the exterminator, from assuming the role of man the restorer in the comeback of this glorious canine.

Make no mistake about it, the wolf has an integral place in the Adirondack landscape. It is the role of top predator—a role not occupied by the coyote or any other species today, despite assertions to the contrary. This role, among other tasks, is critical in supplying a regular source of protein to all lesser predators and scavengers, with all the ramifications entailed in this process.

Today the forest is awaiting the return of a viable wolf population much as it awaits the first cleansing snowfall of winter. Long may its howl be heard and its kind reign in the Great South Woods.

GOLDEN EAGLE

As noble a raptor as graces the skies! Such is a fitting accolade for the golden eagle, which in many respects is truly the king of the air.

It is not the occurrence of this glorious raptor in the Great South Woods that is at issue, but rather the terms of its presence. Is the golden eagle today a truly bona fide resident of the Adirondack Park with a breeding population, or is it merely a vagrant or wandering migrant that no longer claims a permanent place in its ancestral homeland?

Golden eagles are reported regularly locally in all seasons of the year. Winter sightings are, as might be expected, quite sparse. I notice them especially on long canoe trips up the Bog River Flow. They can be seen here soaring over the flow from spring to early autumn. All segments of their population have been noted here, from adults of both genders to immature birds not yet having attained their final plumage. Occasionally, golden eagles are confused with immature bald eagles, but overall there is no doubt about their continued presence.

The last officially confirmed breeding of golden eagles was in the Moose River Plain in the 1970s. Greenleaf Chase and others documented these last known breeding birds. These raptors also possibly bred along the upper Bog River and Lows Lake around that time. Since then there have been plenty of rumors but no direct confirmation of any successful breeding.

The golden eagle, unlike the bald eagle and the osprey, needs extensive open areas as part of its critical habitat in maintaining a population. These large openings should preferably be in proximity to cliffs and ledges for nest sites. Occasionally, those are dispensed with and a large white pine is utilized for the nest.

The open areas are absolutely vital to the golden eagle for successful hunting. Unlike the other two eagles with their preference for fish, the golden eagle is partial to a mammalian prey base. Hares, voles, and woodchucks are all important mainstays in its diet. The marginality of the last known recorded sites in the Great South Woods is evinced by the fact that at the time eagles were last studied, the common bittern and other marsh birds were assuming a major role in their prey base.

There is a dichotomy here. Large, extensive open areas in the Adirondack forest almost invariably result from human activity—fires, clear-cutting, etc.—hardly the stuff of wilderness. With the legal protection afforded the Adirondack Park today by the Adirondack Park Agency (APA) and the high state of effective fire protection attained by the DEC, there appears scant opportunity for such large openings to re-appear in the immediate future. When they do, they are by their very nature only temporal in an area as suited to forest growth as is the Adirondacks. The fire-opened area near Brandon, north of Tupper Lake, is one of the most durable openings around, having come into existence in the early years of the twentieth century. This area too, has been a favorite haunt of the golden eagle.

The "microburst" storm of July 1995 perhaps offers some hope for the golden eagle in the way of openings, or actually semi-openings, as vast multitudes of trees lie crisscrossed everywhere in mostly horizontal positions. Still, there will be a gradual increase in prey population here; this, along with the open spaces for aerial maneuvering that the golden eagle now has, should enhance the bird's status in the Park. Quite possibly this will lead to renewed breeding if in fact the eagle is not now nesting.

Which brings me to the case of Graves Mountain above the Bog River Flow and Lows Lake. For years rumors circulated around Cranberry Lake relative to the existence of a live golden eagle nest on Graves Mountain. Local woodsmen and hunters swore to its being there. This kindled a sense of challenge in me and on three separate occasions I set out to find it. Try as I would, I always seemed to come back empty-handed. The difficulty of the terrain and the broad expanse of its nature were two reasons for this, but added to these were the private posted signs of the Otterbrook Preserve. This proved an insurmountable barrier to my exploring forays as I am old-fashioned enough to be respectful of POSTED signs. I consoled myself at the time and still do now with the thought that some things at sometimes are better off remaining a mystery. How would we have any "creatures of the shadow" otherwise?

Still, I can't help but think that with all the golden eagles out there, it would not be too far-fetched to hope for one solitary nest among them. The microburst could well come to the rescue now.

The golden eagle is different from the bald eagle and from many perspectives it is a much more glorious predator. Long may it soar!

ELK

A creature approaching the ultimate in regalness stood silhouetted majestically against the waning skylight. I stared in total awe until I noticed the ten-foot fence completely encircling the creature's abode. This temporarily put an end to the wild musings of my subconscious!

The creature in question was an American elk. The locale was a farm near Elizabethtown and the year was 1992. I had previously seen elk in farms in the St. Lawrence Valley, but in a background situation not nearly so magnificent. I had also seen their close relative, the European red deer, in the wild in Ireland. Neither of these occasions had induced the flight of fancy inside me that this sighting had awakened from slumber.

The elk has had a quite distinctive and even colorful history in the Great South Woods. There is some controversy as to whether elk were indigenous to the Adirondack Park. What is definitely known is that elk roamed freely throughout the St. Lawrence Valley prior to the coming of Europeans. From here it is presumed that they followed the river valleys up into the Great South Woods. The Grass, Raquette, St. Regis, and Oswegatchie Rivers all had relatively wide valleys with extensive marshes and other open areas—ideal habitat for elk. DeKay, in his classic volume written in 1844 on the mammals of New York, mentioned at least two elk that were shot on the banks of the Raquette River in the vicinity of Saranac Lake. Merriam in his subsequent volume, *Mammals of the Adirondacks,* published in 1882, stated that he had been unable to substantiate these two instances.

Ken Kogut, wildlife biologist of the DEC, seems to concur with Merriam. In the section on wildlife that he authored for the Temporary Study Commission on the Adirondacks in the Twenty-first Century, he recounts receiving a number of inquiries from individuals regarding restoring elk to the Adirondacks. These requests he found "interesting" since no definite specimens of native elk have been recorded in the Adirondacks. As one of those who made these inquiries, I still feel strongly that elk did ascend the north-flowing rivers in colonial times to populate at least the periphery of the Great South Woods. They were not nearly as common as deer or moose, but they did have at least a minor role in the ecosystem of yesterday. A sparing role, but a role nonetheless.

Whatever the situation regarding its status, it is definitely established that native elk had disappeared from the scene before the advent of the nineteenth century.

The distinctiveness and colorfulness of the elk's history in the Great South Woods springs primarily from efforts to reintroduce it to this area. Indeed, for a while, it appeared that efforts at elk restoration had primacy of purpose in the Adirondacks.

These efforts began at the turn of the century when elk and moose were released in the Adirondacks by the old Forestry Commission, one of the precursors of the DEC. The elk did especially well initially and at one time their population increased to around three hundred. At this time efforts at protection were apparently relaxed and the elk gradually met their demise from the bullets of poachers. Some have asserted that the cause of the elk's decline here was the same roundworm harbored by the white-tailed deer that is fatal to moose. I disagree. While this might have played a minor role in reducing the population, the main cause of this initial extirpation was illicit hunting.

The saga continued when the governor of Montana donated a small herd of elk as a gift to the governor of New York. The herd was originally kept in a fenced enclosure near DeBar Mountain. I recall my surprise when I came upon the remnants of this wire fence while researching my *Guide to Adirondack Trails: Northern Region.* The fence still meandered for miles through the forest. These elk gradually escaped their enclosure and spread out locally through the forest. They lasted until the late 1950s, according to an article in the *New York Fish and Game Journal.* Again, sporadic efforts at protection were probably the main culprit. The elk spread into St. Lawrence County also, and one was killed on the grounds of the Stillwater Club in the 1930s. A substantial fine was paid. One animal was killed by a prominent Manhattanite in the late 1940s on the grounds of the august North Woods Club. He alleged he mistook it for a deer. For his misidentification he paid a hefty fine.

The final attempt at restoring elk was undertaken under wholly private auspices. Litchfield Park and Whitney Park both had released elk along with other species in this effort in the 1930s. These elk spread more widely than those of the prior attempts. By 1940 they ranged through wide areas of the St. Lawrence, Franklin, and Hamilton County portions of the Great South Woods. A small herd resulting from this effort was featured in a prominent photograph in one of the late Barney Fowler's *Adirondack Albums.*

An onslaught was also undertaken against these elk during World War II and shortly thereafter. There were rumors of the Benevolent & Protective Order of Elks offering up to $200 for the unique incisor teeth of the elk. The race was on. It centered around Tupper Lake and extended down to the vicinity of Little Tupper Lake where the herd photographed in Fowler's book lived. An elk was reportedly seen by numerous individuals on the south shore of Cranberry Lake around 1960, also the time that Environmental Conservation Officer Bruce Perry of Long Lake informed me that he saw one in the town of Hopkinton in St. Lawrence County. For all practical purposes the history of the Adirondack elk came to a conclusion circa 1960.

Has the final curtain truly fallen, however? In 1993 a friend found a perfect set of elk antlers while canoeing a remote area of the Little River near Aldrich during a hunting expedition. With the brief existence that fallen cerrid antlers invariably have because small rodents and porcupines crave sodium, it is highly unlikely that the antlers had lain there for any length of time. The locale where the antlers lay was deep in the Forest Preserve, far from any camp that the antlers could have adorned as a trophy. The only logical explanation is either a hoax played on the finder (which I consider unlikely) or an escape from one of the game farms. Still, it had the effect of stirring my imagination.

I'd like to see elk present once again in the Great South Woods. I believe there is a definite role for them in this more enlightened era. Their presence, while being subordinate to that of deer and moose, would be a stirring sight for all who viewed them and would also be a living representation of a past era in the Great South Woods.

LYNX

It was just before dusk settled on the waning of a sultry August day that I had my first personal encounter with one of the "creatures of the shadow." The creature in question was a Canada lynx and the location was the highway between Tupper Lake and Long Lake. The year was 1977.

The carcass of a road-killed deer lay in the middle of the highway. Standing over the deer and feeding as contentedly as a kitten partaking of house chow on her remains stood a breathtaking Canada lynx. The long legs and huge feet made her seem almost a parody and the awkward gait she utilized in scrambling to the edge of the road only confirmed this initial impression. This was completely eclipsed by the overriding aura of majesty and wildness that she still managed to convey.

One moment she stood there and gave a cat-like glance in my direction; the next moment she was gone. She appeared to vanish into the bowels of the forest. No wonder cats have this reputation for spookiness!

A survey of the deer carcass disclosed that the lynx had only just commenced to feed. The sense of regret I felt at this was much overshadowed by the feeling of awe and wonderment that the cat left me with. This feeling has not receded in the slightest with the passage of the years.

Up to the time of the sighting I had assumed Canada lynx to be a creature of the past in New York. A little research established that such was not exactly the case. Lynx appeared to turn up sporadically but regularly in the Adirondacks. From 1950 to 1975 at least five were documented, with a number of them being turned in to collect the bounty on bobcats that still existed locally. Bounties are now, fortunately, a part of the past but it is interesting to conjecture if any more lynx were harvested and mistakenly identified as bobcats.

One of those harvested was shot by a rabbit hunter near Croghan. The mounted specimen, which this subsequently became, was exhibited at Jefferson Community College in Watertown for a number of years. I was fortunate enough to view this specimen while it was still displayed.

Several lynx were taken in the central Adirondacks, including one near Indian Lake. These last cats were documented as Canada lynx only after they had been presented to government agencies to collect the official bounty.

The last lynx taken in the Adirondacks was trapped in Altona on the eastern side of the mountain. This was immediately prior to the Canada lynx being accorded complete protection in the state of New York.

The prevailing theory holds that bobcats displaced the Canada lynx in the Great South Woods with the advent of extensive timber harvesting. This had the effect of increasing deer populations, thereby providing additional winter nutrients for bobcat, that are far more adept at killing deer than lynx.

The growth of the Forest Preserve probably provided one of the incentives for an official effort at restoration undertaken in the late 1980s by the SUNY College of Environmental Science and Forestry field station in Newcomb. Perhaps this effort should have been termed an enhancement of a tenuous existing population rather than a reintroduction of an extirpated species.

The stock for this restoration came from the far-away Yukon Territory. The Yukon has few roads where lynx could become street-wise, and some have suggested that this was the main reason for the high road mortality of the introduced felines. It probably played a role, but the history of the reintroduction of large carnivores is replete with stories of initial high mortality from road fatalities. This is primarily due to the penchant for wide-spread wandering inherent in large carnivores. This is especially notable in animals that are temporarily disoriented after a translocation effort. Attempts at restoring black bear to Arkansas and bobcat to New Jersey were at first presumed to be failures due to the high mortality at the outset thanks to this penchant for wandering. Subsequent events revealed that the efforts had in fact been successful in re-establishing populations of these two indigenous species.

How our Canada lynx did wander! New Hampshire, Binghamton—no place in the East appeared to be immune from the reach of their sojourning. But some seem to have taken hold. I've begun to see lynx tracks in the winter deer yards east of Cranberry Lake. A lynx was seen shortly thereafter in the same vicinity by a number of individuals. However, no collar that would indicate one of the translocated cats was apparent. This, therefore, was a lynx whose collar had fallen off or one whose presence was not the result of the reintroduction attempt. The latter translates to a bona fide native Adirondacker!

In 1994 a report was received by the Endangered Species Unit of the DEC located in Delmar of the presence of a Canada lynx with the radio collar still intact. The locale of this sighting was the High Peaks region, the site of the original release of the lynx.

The question arises: does any ecosystem have room for three species of wild cats? The Great South Woods and the Adirondacks in general just might be one of the few ecosystems that does. With its conifer swamps and hardwood hills interspersed liberally and supporting a varied prey base, this area seems to offer something for all three cats. If all three felines are to have viable populations, the wholehearted participation of the DEC will be essential. There was somewhat of a tiff over turf, so to speak, in the restoration effort sponsored by SUNY ESF. This must not be allowed to repeat itself!

May the presence of a creature that so much typifies the wilderness of boreal climes always grace our forests.

COUGAR

The "phantom of the mountains"—if ever there were truly such a title it surely must go to this cryptic long-tailed feline, that is beyond question the premier "creature of the shadows." Generations of residents of the Great South Woods have whispered in awe about its presence. A multitude of written material has been produced relative to its status and a considerable amount of effort has been expended on safaris of sorts to prove or disprove its existence. None have been able to confirm or, for that matter, repudiate the possibility. The rumors in fact appear to have proliferated. Some local woodsmen, when in the company of kindred spirits, have actually begun to raise their voices above the whisper stage.

I became aware of these purported sightings of this mystery cat almost immediately upon arriving in the Adirondacks. Many close personal friends as well as a host of acquaintances have claimed to have seen cougars over the past several decades. A number of times while winter tracking I have come upon what I feel could be nothing else except cougar tracks.

One memorable occurrence was an instance with DEC Forest Ranger John Hurlbut. I was skiing in to Streeter Lake when I came upon two clear, distinct feline tracks—one large and one small. I called John (now a lieutenant) and asked him to bring a camera since the tracks were vividly etched on a newly-made snowmobile base. However, the North Country did as it is often wont to do and by the time John arrived with the camera another inch of snow had dropped, effectively obliterating or at least obscuring the tracks. Still, we enjoyed following them through the snow. The long tail was clearly reflected in a number of places on the snow and there was also a spot where one of the cats had meticulously scooped out a shallow hole in the snow and delicately delivered her spoor there. I say "her" because we had come to the conclusion that we were dealing with a mother cougar and her half-grown cub.

On another occasion, at Long Pond deep in the Aldrich Pond Wild Forest, a walking feline leaving a 3½-inch circular track on the iced surface of the pond suddenly made a twenty-three-foot leap, apparently from a standing position. This fact was clearly revealed in the thin film of snow overlaying the ice. From here the enigmatic cat vented its rage on the frozen muck of a beaver lodge on the shore. It strove mightily but was unable to rip apart the lodge and secure access to the slumbering beaver therein.

The official position today, and for a long time conventional wisdom as well, decrees that the cougar became extirpated in the Adirondacks around 1900. Pivotal in their disappearance, or at least decline, were the efforts of varied and sundry woodsmen seeking to secure the generous bounty that then existed for producing evidence of a dead cougar. Chief among the cougar's nemeses here was the colorful George Muir of the town of Fine. George waited until winter and then proceeded to take his specially trained dog pack out for a cruise until they came across a relatively fresh track of a cougar. He then set loose the dogs, who followed the tracks and scent until they invariably treed the now forlorn feline. This usually occurred sooner rather than later as the howling and other oral din made by the dogs apparently stimulated the cougar to seek safety (or what appeared to be such) in a suitable tree.

The reaction of the cougar to the dogs, which it could easily have decimated individually or even as a small pack, is interesting. Mammalogists have speculated that in the past cougars had a canine foe for which this manner of escape behavior was suitable. This role was probably played by the dire wolf, a canid considerably larger than today's timber wolf, which became extinct as the last Ice Age ground to a close. After dispatching the cougar, George would detach a part of the carcass, often an ear, and bring it to the nearest town clerk in order to obtain the bounty.

George has descendants in the area today and they often talk about

him with pride. Times were different then, and activities that are
frowned on today fit in with the tenor of that era.

All alleged sightings up to a decade ago were attributable to simple
misidentifications. Fisher, bear, large feral house cats, all were prof-
fered as explanations, as was the possibility of plain old hallucinations.
About this time a distinct shift in the attitude and response of the DEC
to reported sightings of cougars became evident. Henceforth, most
sightings of large long-tailed cats were to be attributable to "escaped"
and/or "released" individuals.

Perhaps this shift in attitude was in response to the numerous reports of sightings by their own personnel that began to filter in. I have
been personally informed by no fewer than seven present or former
employees of the DEC that they have witnessed what only could be
bona fide cougars or panthers prancing in the wild. These direct sightings were usually made by field personnel in the course of their regular
activities. The twelve-week-old cougar kitten shot by a bobcat hunter
in 1993 when treed by his dogs, as well as the adult cougar found dead
at the bottom of a gorge in 1968, presumably also spring from this
"escaped" or "released" source. The former took place near Sacandaga
while the latter was in the vicinity of Saranac Lake. When we add to
these the two "escaped" cougars reported by Paul Rezendes in his book
on winter tracking as having been recorded by the Warrensburg Office
of the DEC, we see clearly illuminated the ironic fact that these several
misplaced cats seem to possess a decided penchant to turn up in one of
the wildest places in the East when they escape from captivity!

Being by nature and career programmed to be a trusting sort, I now
began to entertain some doubts about the wisdom of officialdom in this
matter. Research on the subject disclosed an uninterrupted string of
claimed cougar sightings dating back to the time of the fabled Adirondack hermit Noah Rondeau in the 1920s. Furthermore, there were three
feature articles in the DEC's official *New York State Conservationist*
magazine during the 1950s alluding mostly in the affirmative to the
question of the "panther's" presence in the Adirondacks during this
period. (The cougar is also called the panther, puma, painter, and mountain lion.)

Even more astounding was the fact that I soon discovered that a
similar situation existed in all the wild, wooded areas of the entire east-

ern United States. Whether Maine, Vermont, New Hampshire, or Pennsylvania, the tale had a familiar ring to it: numerous valid sightings of cougars but all presumed to emanate from individual cats formerly in captivity!

I eventually became affiliated with a group, the Eastern Puma Research Network, which has been documenting reports of cougars and/ or panthers from all over the East during the past two decades. Their files disclose not only thousands of alleged sightings by reputable sources during this period but also a number of cougars definitely being killed in the eastern states. As in the Adirondacks, the Fish and Wildlife departments of the various states involved attributed all these individuals to escaped stock.

The unanimity of opinion regarding this matter is quite interesting and unusual. Could we, perchance, be dealing with more than meets the eye?

As I began to accumulate reports, a number of interesting facts became readily evident almost from the outset. One of these was the number of prominent Adirondackers who have claimed to see cougars in a wild state locally. These range from naturalist and author Ed Reid to the foremost Adirondack plant ecologist, Ed Ketchledge. Barbara McMartin, the author and editor, also informed me that she saw one of these enigmatic felines. Not to mention the scores of sighting reports I received from the every-day Adirondacker. The sightings came from all over the Great South Woods and the entire Adirondack Park. There was a heavy concentration of these reports near the Five Ponds Wilderness and adjacent wild forests. Privately-owned Whitney Park was also the locale of many sightings. Other areas which appeared to have a greater-than-average number of sightings were the axis from Tupper and Saranac Lakes over to Long Lake and also the area around Keene Valley.

Another interesting aspect of the reports is the number of kittens that people claimed to see in the company of adult cougars. These seem to me a strong refutation of the "escape" theory as the sole source of cougar sightings. Several DEC officers, including Bruce Perry of Long Lake and Frank Morehouse of North Creek, informed me of reports of cougar offspring they had received which they considered valid.

Then there was the case of the white-tailed doe twenty feet up in the crotch of a sugar maple one wintry snow-laden January day near Tupper Lake. Ranger Joe Kennedy of Piercefield reported this to me and spoke of his beliefs as to how the deer got up the tree. This storing of a prey carcass high up in a tree to secure it from competing scavengers is a fairly common tactic resorted to by cougars in the Northwest. With packs of the large Eastern coyotes with their ravenous appetites abundant locally, it would seem to be logical for our area's cats to adopt a similar strategy.

Baxter Mountain, near Keene Valley, was the site of an excellent series of videos of a deer carcass which had been clearly killed and partially consumed by a cougar. In addition to the tooth and claw marks, the carcass was almost completely covered with leaves and other debris in the classic cougar fashion. Another video of the same situation was taken forty miles north of this site a few days following. The only question remaining relative to these occurrences is whether one cougar or two separate ones were involved.

Whether the cougars that all involved concede are being seen are remnants of an indigenous population or, alternately, descend from "escaped" individuals, is much more than academic. The original cougar population of the East—*Felis concolor cougar*—has been officially designated an endangered species by the federal government. As such certain stringent and determined efforts must be made to protect this subspecies and restore it to viable numbers.

Therein might possibly lie the reluctance of our DEC and the wildlife agencies of adjoining states to recognize the individuals being sighted by so many as authentic descendants of an indigenous population. The "Florida Panther"—*Felis concolor conyi*—is also designated a federal endangered species. Untold millions of dollars have been expended in the effort to protect it and the critical wildlife habitat it is dependent on. Should not such efforts also be mandated locally? One can imagine what would ensue in the way of controversy in the wake of such efforts! Guess who would be right in the middle? I imagine I've become a bit of a cynic in this matter, but my cynicism is increasingly reflected by other environmentalists regarding this subject.

A fascinating highlight concerning these sightings is the number of individuals reporting that they have seen jet-black, large, long-tailed cats. The Eastern Puma Research Network estimates that approximately 25% of the sightings reported to them fit into this category. The percentage reported locally to me is somewhat lower that this, but still quite considerable.

What can the above mean? According to scientific records there has been only one confirmed, documented specimen of a black (melanistic) cougar ever recorded. That was in South America several generations ago.

What exactly are we dealing with here? Could an isolated eastern population have developed a genetic trait for melanism in response to the isolation and the forested habitat generally prevailing? Or are we dealing with something entirely different, an unrecorded variety at least of escaped exotics that have somehow established a population, at least tenuously?

I do know those reporting these sightings to me are definite in their assessment of skin color. These black cats appear, on the average, to be somewhat smaller than the tawny ones. In addition, a number of those reporting claim that the felines they observed had red eyes. This has never been claimed, as far as I know, in regard to the tawny individuals purportedly seen. While no employees of the DEC have reported black individuals to me, I do have reports from both a clergyman and a state trooper on patrol, among others, relative to the occurrence of these "black panthers."

The possible existence of large black cats adds even more mystery to this subject. A miniature riddle, so to speak, wrapped in the overall puzzle of the existence of the cougar. It certainly stirs the imagination!

It is a common belief that cats have nine lives. The cryptic nature of the cougar's presence in the Great South Woods and other wild areas of the East is ample testimony to its tenacity. Still, its time of re-emergence from the shadows may be near at hand. I certainly hope so.

IV

THE DEER YARD

Photo by Gerry Lemmo
Lake with fringing trees

Traditionally, the white-tailed deer is the wildlife species people most associate with the Adirondacks. Economically it must certainly be given pride of place.

At one time early in the twentieth century, deer in New York State were virtually restricted to the Adirondacks as a consequence of intensive agriculture and market hunting elsewhere in the state. This is ironic since originally the Adirondacks were only marginal deer habitat, conditions being generally better suited for moose. The heavy cutting of the Adirondack conifer forest and the eventual re-vegetation by hardwood scrub and saplings provided the impetus for a veritable explosion in the deer population. The virtual elimination of the large predators also helped matters along.

Today there is still a limiting factor that makes the Adirondacks only a moderately productive deer range. During an average Adirondack winter, the intense cold and deep snow are often too severe for deer to prosper. The nutritious hardwood browse which has sustained throughout the fall is often not adequate to maintain the metabolic rate and basic body function of the average deer in winter.

As the snow slowly and inexorably piles ever higher on the ground, there comes a time when the energy a beleaguered white-tailed deer must expend to plow through it is simply not worth the effort. In the Adirondacks the critical snow depth is generally fifteen to twenty inches depending on variables including, among others, the prior condition of the deer and the texture of the snow.

Now the deer must begin a trek of upwards of ten miles to find an area better suited to harboring them from the brutal elements of winter. In the northwestern Adirondack area, low-lying conifer swamps, often fringing rivers and lakes, are usually the chosen site. It now becomes the deer yard or winter concentration area. Here, under the protective cover of sheltering evergreens, the deer find relief from the fierce, desiccating winds of winter. In addition, the shallower and usually harder-packed snow cover makes it easier for the deer to tread through the yard without expending excess energy.

But paradise is not without its pitfalls, in this instance the lack of nutritious food in or adjacent to the conifer swamps. Most conifer species are either unpalatable to deer or offer insufficient nutrient levels to enable them to withstand the rigors of winter. There are two exceptions: white cedar and eastern hemlock, both deer favorites. Unfortunately, they are sparse in certain areas of the Adirondacks.

Even though abundant hardwood browse may be only a short distance away, as the winter progresses and the snow remains deep, the deer stay close to the yard and slowly succumb to starvation. Many biologists consider sixty days of deep snow the critical point after which significant mortality begins.

As the deer begin dying, the deer yard becomes host to a broad array of species. It is now truly the focal point for beleaguered winter wildlife for miles around. A spectrum of predators and scavengers converge, seeking sustenance from the deer carcasses as the toll begins to mount. They are a diverse lot. In addition to the traditional predators there are also others not normally considered meat eaters who change their habits under winter's stressful conditions. This roster may include red and flying squirrels, woodpeckers, chickadees, gray and blue jays, and others as well.

The deer yard closest to my home, and the one with which I am most familiar, is designated officially by the New York State DEC as the Dead Creek Yard. It lies east of the hamlet of Cranberry Lake and stretches from the Oswegatchie River across the South Branch of the Grass River and all the way to the banks of the Raquette River. This is classic "yard" country with extensive conifer flats in the lowlands providing protection from the wind and cold, and wooded adjacent hardwood knolls furnishing nutritious browse. Sporadic artificial feeding of corn and alfalfa by several local hunting clubs also serves as additional sustenance for the deer. They often use the rivers themselves as passageways, probably gaining an added sense of security from the firmer footing provided by the river ice.

Dead Creek Yard is the site of an annual survey conducted in early April to determine the extent of mortality during the previous winter season. The survey is then used as one indicator to help reveal the significance of deer kill for all the yards in this region of the Adirondacks. Deer harvest seasons are then set accordingly. For over a decade I have been privileged to participate in this survey, from which I have learned a startling number of facts.

As might be expected, the amount of deer mortality varies dramatically from winter to winter depending on the severity of the season. I have seen the kill fluctuate from approximately a score to several hundred. Inevitably, fawns of the current season are the first to die, and if the winter is a relatively open and mild one, mortality may actually end here. Biologists can frequently determine the cause of death by cracking open the thighbone with a small hand ax. A red or strawberry color without any trace of white indicates the deer has used up all its fat reserves and has probably succumbed to starvation or to a related condition resulting from inadequate nutrition. Death by direct predation can also usually, though not always, be determined. In any event, usually all the carcasses have been scavenged, some lightly, some completely.

With the arrival of the predators and attendant scavengers, the deer yard begins to assume a special aura. For while the presence of deer may give definition to the yard, it is the predators that impart the sense of allure that bestows on deer yards their truly unique quality. Whether in pursuit of prey of merely scavenging carrion, these dramatic predators convey a sense of excitement all too rare in this otherwise tame world.

Foremost among the predators is the enigmatic Eastern coyote. While there may be some debate as to the origin and genetic composition of this canid, even extending to the question of whether different "types" or even species are involved, there is none whatsoever concerning the role of this animal in the winter deer yard. This canine appears to form packs in the winter specifically for the purpose of preying on deer. The nutrition derived from preying and scavenging on deer enables the Eastern coyote not only to survive the winter but also to mate successfully during the latter part of the season.

The packs formed by this larger version of the Western coyote are variable in number, usually consisting of family groupings. I have seen packs with as many as nine in the Adirondacks, although larger ones may exist.

Scavenging becomes more important as the winter progresses and deer mortality increases due to starvation and related causes. The pack usually depends on a chase to secure the deer. Deep, soft snow often works in their favor as it severely hampers the deer's progress more than the canids'. On the other hand, the strength of the crust may offer an edge to either the coyote or the deer. When the snow is soft and fluffy, deer often seek the more secure footing of river and lake ice; and it is in these venues that I have witnessed two actual deer kills.

One was on a flow of Cranberry Lake while the other was on the South Branch of the Grass River. Both were truly awesome spectacles that I came upon as they were concluding; each is vividly etched forever in my memory. In both instances, the coyote attacked from the rear and appeared to hamstring the deer. Both times the deer found the ice more slippery and limiting to rapid flight than did the canids. In one case I arrived immediately after the kill, although I had witnessed part of the actual chase itself. The one regret I have concerning both incidents was that my arrival frightened the coyotes, who departed without feeding on their hard-won trophies.

With their strong teeth and jaws, coyotes will frequently tear chunks of meat and limbs from a carcass and take them to a more secluded area for further ingestion. This is commonplace when the carcass is in a spot vulnerable to pilferage by other predators and scavengers. Often coyotes move under a windfall or to the midst of thick conifer growth — as hidden a nook and cranny as can be found in the woods. When prey is scarce, the carcass may be consumed so thoroughly that it is reduced to a pile of hair. In addition to deer, snowshoe hare, which are often abundant in the yards because of the ideal habitat provided by the low conifer growth, are regularly preyed on by the coyotes.

The myriad of lesser predators that seems to flow in the wake of the coyote packs are now very much in evidence. In fact, some of them actually follow the packs seeking to share some of their bounty. However we may view this as illicit and unearned, it is actually all part of the Creator's grand design of waste-not and an integral strand of the winter ecological web. To thwart these camp followers, then, the coyote secures portions of its prey in secluded areas much as its relative, the domestic dog, will bury its bone.

In the Adirondacks, this legion of pack camp followers runs the gamut from foxes and weasels to ravens, jays, and bald eagles. All seek a piece of the proverbial pie, in this case venison. The red foxes and the occasional gray fox found in the deer yard use the deer carcasses mainly to supplement their regular fare of snowshoe hare.

The number of bobcats in the winter deer yards fluctuates dramatically. Some years they are barely present while in others their tracks are a regular part of the landscape. Whatever their numbers, it is axiomatic among Adirondack woodsmen that any local bobcats will automatically take up residence in the nearest deer yard during the winter months. Bobcats generally utilize carrion only as a last resort, but that often comes to pass in a typical Adirondack winter.

Bobcats, usually solitary at this time of year, often kill deer in the yards. They do this by attacking the deer after a stealthy, protracted stalk as the deer lie in their beds. The deer are then dispatched by bites and some blows to the head and neck areas. All four of the winter-killed deer that I could positively determine were dispatched by bob-cats were killed in this fashion. Of the four, two were large adults. In only one instance was an attempt made to cover the carcass in the tradi-tionally prescribed manner attributed to bobcats. Snow was strewn across the carcass in such a way that the effect was a striking mosaic of gray and white on the forest floor.

The relatively few lynx in the Adirondacks are also attracted to the deer yards. The only set of tracks of this glorious feline I have come across in the Dead Creek Yard was deliberately proceeding from deer carcass to deer carcass, sampling a portion of each. Of course, lynx prey as heavily on snowshoe hares during the winter as they do in other seasons of the year. If not, their huge snow-adapted paws would appear to be totally redundant at this time of year!

The members of the weasel clan, which is large and quite varied in the Adirondacks, are naturally well represented in the deer yards. The largest local representative is the striking and dramatic fisher. In winter their tracks lace up and down the deer yards in a tireless probing for carrion and snowshoe hares to tide them through the season. Fisher usually have arboreal dens and regularly climb trees to dispatch a fa-vorite prey, the porcupine. However, in my experience they are mostly terrestrial. In March, the tracks of the smaller females appear in tandem with the males. I recently observed a fisher driving a red fox from a deer carcass before the fox had finished eating. The fox matched the fisher in size and appetite, perhaps, but certainly not in ferocity. I re-member the frigid, wintry, mid-April Tug Hill day in 1972, when a companion and I, following fisher tracks, came upon a fox den dug in the snow. Strewn around the den were the remains of four fox kits, ap-parently killed but not eaten by the fisher. The evidence did not explain whether the vixen had been present at the time, but if so, we could only conclude that she hastily abandoned the den to the rage of the fisher.

Mink also leave their tracks in the deer yard in winter, seeking nu-trients often far from their usual aquatic haunts. Both mink and fisher can occasionally be seen hunting abroad on cloudy days during this season of want.

I do not often see the track of the pine marten at this time of year in the deer yards. Apparently their habit of foraging under the snow cover for voles and shrews during this season means they need not rely exclusively on the conifer cover of the deer yards to be successful.

The smallest local members of the clan are quite a different proposition. The long-tailed weasel and the ermine, both now resplendent in their coats of winter white, positively haunt the deer yards during this season. Their tracks are seemingly everywhere, going under the snow pack for voles and exploring apertures in the snow at the base of the trees for deer mice. At the same time, their tracks often lead directly to the nearest deer carcass. One memorable sight I'll forever treasure is that of an ermine who took up residence in the cadaver of an expired deer. There it fed away to its heart's content, entirely oblivious to all transpiring around it. From its perspective, the abundant proteins it wallowed amidst in what usually would be its time of want must have appeared to be a weasel's heaven. When I prodded the carcass with my snowshoes, the ermine would promptly peek out from the stomach cavity to gaze at me and just as promptly withdraw again into the recesses of its paradise!

The Adirondacks' largest predator, the black bear, provides us with a much different scenario. Actually omnivores, bears usually doze away in hibernation during this time of winter scarcity. However, in years with severe winters and correspondingly high deer mortality, bears, too, will seek sustenance in the deer yards when they awaken from their slumber. This generally occurs around mid-April and they will promptly proceed to clean up any carcasses still remaining. If the deer is a recent casualty, the bears will simply use their mighty strength to cart the whole carcass off. I felt a profound sense of wonder when I first noticed these disappearing carcasses, until I finally realized what was happening.

Predation and scavenging in the deer yards are not solely restricted to the mammals. Members of the tribe of feathered predators who remain through the winter are also wont to congregate around deer yards. Ravens flock here for their supply of nutrients. I have seen as many as eleven take flight from a single deer carcass. Highly intelligent, they post sentinels to give an alarm while feeding and actually appear to follow the coyote packs in their daily patrols. These actions, together with the eerie, discordant sounds they utter, give credence to Edgar Allen Poe's depiction of them as the symbol of evil in his epic poem.

That other black, corvid symbol of malice, the crow, usually leaves our area in winter to fly north a few miles to the St. Lawrence Valley. The lesser snow cover there, along with standing corn stalks, enables crows to survive. However, during several recent mild winters crows have stayed put and added their presence to the local deer yard congregation.

Also quite recently, that monarch of the American skies, the bald eagle, has begun to maintain a presence in the winter yards. The abundant deer carcasses apparently provide an adequate substitute for the eagles' usual fare of fish. Three to six eagles have taken up residence between Dead Creek Yard and nearby Carry Falls Reservoir. I have observed both adult and immature eagles watching ravens discover a carcass and then proceed to hone in on it while unceremoniously driving away the loudly protesting ravens. Their feeding signs are dramatically distinct from those of ravens. The strong beaks and claws of eagles literally tear flesh from the carcass of the dead deer as opposed to the neat, precise, small feeding holes of the much more feeble-beaked raven. The raven invariably pecks out the eyes before beginning to feed—another reminder of the dark mystique enshrouding these birds!

Red-tailed hawks, too, will take up residence in a deer yard when they first return to the Adirondacks in late March or early April. Unforgettable is the spectacle of one of these noble raptors making repeated passes at the ermine hiding in the cavity of a deer carcass, in a vain attempt to turn that smaller predator into prey.

At long last the day arrives when the snow pack begins to decline rapidly with the advent of rising temperatures and longer spring days. Now the deer begin their annual odyssey from the deer yard back to their traditional summer range. With the departure of the deer, the artificially high population of predators and scavengers also dramatically declines.

Recent research conducted at Newcomb in the central Adirondacks by SUNY ESF has revealed that these age-old migratory patterns are deeply embedded in the memory of the white-tailed deer, having been adhered to for countless generations. This research has also uncovered another interesting factor which may have relevance for the human species. These ancient patterns turn out to have a strong matriarchal basis: the does lead their fawns of the present year, plus their female yearlings, into their specific yards while yearling males follow the does, whose orbit they have encountered, into their traditional yards. Whether relevant for humankind or not, this does provide a concise illustration of one manner in which Mother Nature has erected another barrier to inbreeding, thus providing for the genetic diversity that ultimately benefits all her creatures.

V

THE BEAVER POND

Beaver eating bark off branch

If the Adirondack deer yard is the center of the universe as regards wildlife activity during winter, surely pride of place in summer must go to the beaver pond. This wildlife utopia begins when a dam is erected across a generally small, usually level or only slightly inclined creek, by an industrious beaver. The ingredients used in the dam's erection are varied—mud, boulders, but most of all wood from a variety of tree species. The result is an almost instant pond sprawling across the landscape and the setting in motion of a process of altering and diversifying that landscape through a series of gradual changes of habitat.

The main impetus for the creation of the pond stems from the desire of the beaver to increase its food supply and at the same time provide the aquatic security that it so cherishes. Whatever the reasons, one fact is as crystal clear as an Adirondack creek: the vicinity of these beaver ponds is as much the hub of wildlife activity when the forest floor is laced with green as it is in winter when the same floor is coated with a mantle of white.

The reasons for the appeal of beaver ponds to wildlife are many. The primary one, encompassing all the others, is the multitude of varied habitats ultimately created by the erection of the dam. The immediate area becomes, over time, a shifting mosaic of pond to marsh to meadow and eventually returns to forest. Often all components are adjacent to one another simultaneously, depending on the beavers' level of activity on different stretches of the stream. The progression from an aquatic to a terrestrial state continues as the principle of ecological succession asserts itself after the beavers' withdrawal from the area.

A secondary reason for the beaver pond's importance to wildlife is the creation of an ecotone effect as areas of forest come to border on water and open areas. Ecotones, areas of contact between two different habitats, are invariably richer in wildlife diversity than are single habitats. This is so because they usually possess their own distinctive species in addition to some of those of the adjoining habitats.

Add to the above the fact that beaver ponds and their successive stages are frequently the only openings for miles around in the Adirondack forest and it becomes evident that these ponds are absolutely vital to wildlife diversity and numbers in the Great South Woods.

The change in wildlife begins almost immediately. The flooded, dead trees become nesting sites for tree swallows, kingbirds, crested fly-catchers, and flickers among others. I have often seen the bluebird, the symbol of New York State, nesting in the holes and hollows of dead trees on beaver ponds many miles from the nearest open areas. Is this a case of the bluebird adjusting to a newly created niche, or simply a reversion to a trait that was prevalent in primeval times before the advent of ornithologists? I often wonder.

The change in fauna becomes more pronounced as the pond takes shape and sprawls over the surrounding land. The existing forested habitat is effectively transformed into an aquatic community. A proliferation of life forms that ranges from tiny microorganisms in the pond to dramatic vertebrates also in and beside the pond now seems to spring forth miraculously. The rapid increase in aquatic food of all kinds is reflected in an upswing in populations as diverse as the hordes of dragonflies swarming above the pond on a bright sunlit day and the voracious brook trout swimming in its depths, more active on cloudy days.

The subject of brook trout and beaver ponds has long been controversial in the Adirondacks. The bone of contention revolves around whether beaver ponds enhance or detract from the quality of brook trout fishing. Each of these opposing viewpoints has its own ardent supporters who would no more give credence to the other point of view than they would use a net to harvest these same trout. My own experience has been that some of the most dynamic Adirondack fishing can be had by standing on the dam of a tiny beaver pond and casting a worm into its depths. This is soulful and productive, even taking into account the numerous horned dace that are also taken along with the trout. The steep increase in food abundance that occurs initially as the small stream changes into an expansive pond accounts for this spurt in numbers of the local trout population.

I have noticed, however, that as the pond ages and inevitably begins to warm, brook trout numbers invariably begin to decrease. The warming process is often inaugurated by the toppling of the flooded trees and the ensuing increased exposure of the pond to the full brunt of the sun's rays. The gradual buildup of silt at the pond's edges that occurs naturally with the passage of time also contributes to the process of warming. Brook trout have a love affair with clear, cold water and there is a temperature comfort level above which they will not thrive. In addition, the buildup of silt often obliterates the gravel beds that are necessary for the autumn spawning of the trout. In any event, I have noticed that trout numbers inevitably seem to peak early in the life of a beaver pond and then gradually begin to decline as the pond ages and the waters become warmer.

One thing is certain: the dams themselves do not inhibit brook trout in the least from swimming through them, as was once widely believed. On several occasions I've watched brook trout go right through a dam without even so much as breaking stride.

When we come to the architect of this faunal heaven—can enough be said of the beaver? The largest rodent in North America, an engineer extraordinaire and a practitioner of monogamy in spousal relationships, the beaver was chosen as the New York State Mammal. Some see it rivaling the bald eagle as the national emblem.

Beaver were the preferred target of fur trappers in colonial times. For almost a century they were practically extirpated in the Adirondacks. They became re-established around 1910 when stock was secured from Yellowstone Park to supplement the remaining few native beaver in the St. Regis River and perhaps the Oswegatchie drainage.

I have heard of beaver weighing close to ninety pounds but the largest I have ever seen was trapped by a friend in the town of Fine, in 1980, that came in at seventy-two pounds on two different scales.

Beavers usually mate for life, with up to three generations residing as a colony in a pond. The two-year-old kits are driven from the pond about the time in February that the young of the current year come forth. The expelled kits then commence wandering until they find a stretch of unoccupied brook for their own. During these wanderings they exhibit a propensity to turn up in the most unlikely locations. Even knowing this, I am still startled when I see them in the middle of an Adirondack hamlet, as I have on several occasions.

An engineer extraordinaire the beaver may be, but I can't help but wonder how much of this is pure instinct rather than design? For instance, fully one-third of the large trees I have seen cut locally wind up hanging across other trees rather than falling on the ground. At best this is a supreme waste of effort. At worst the trees topple onto the beaver himself, leading to the early demise of the "engineer." Still and all, a remarkable creature!

I've not only watched brook trout swim through a beaver dam, but also a stray otter or two. In the otter we have a species whose relation to a beaver pond can be likened to a match made in paradise. Otters thrive here, perhaps attaining their ultimate in numbers around beaver ponds. Fish, mussels, crayfish, frogs all see their populations explode when a beaver pond comes into existence. All are fodder for a famished otter.

The beaver lodge itself, both active and abandoned, is often utilized by otter as both a den and a resting area. I frequently come upon otters resting on both lodges and large boulders in ponds. Like a flash they plunge into the water. An imposing sight indeed, but nothing like the sight of an otter flowing onto a log in one sinuous motion; the mounting of the floating log is done in a seemingly effortless fashion and never ceases to amaze me. Otter and log appear to assume one form!

Family groups of otter are particularly in evidence in autumn. They can be seen with their heads bobbing in and out of the water, all the while uttering a creaking, plaintive call. Both sight and sound here, once experienced, will be long retained in memory. Visions of mermaids and "Champ," the mythical Lake Champlain monster, are invoked while viewing this performance. Who knows?

Mink, too, are common around beaver ponds. They are attracted not only by the increase in the aquatic food supply, but also by a pronounced proliferation of small mammals that inhabit the open area created by the beaver's felling of trees adjacent to the pond. I often see them hunting on cloudy days as much for voles on land as for frogs on the edge of the pond. Mink also use the beaver lodge for den sites, but not to the extent that otters appear to. They seem especially tame when alighting from the water. A number of times they have run right past me without so much as a glance in my direction. I have often enjoyed the entrancing sight of a harried mink abroad on a cloudy day being followed by a phalanx of blue jays who are proceeding to vent all their considerable venom in the direction of the forlorn mink. While not lessening their vocalization one whit, they somehow manage to continually dive bomb the object of their rage. I imagine they're merely returning past favors rendered by the mink!

Raccoons also find beaver ponds irresistible and proliferate in their vicinity. An increased food supply is part of the reason. Raccoons delight in mussels, crayfish, the eggs of water birds and other tidbits so common around these ponds. Equally compelling for 'coons is the abundance of den sites provided by the many standing dead trees. The raccoon, although heavily built, is quite deceptive in its ability to squeeze through even relatively modest-sized holes in trees. I often watch them exiting from openings in hollow dead trees ringing beaver ponds. A few times the hole was no larger than one made by a pileated woodpecker.

With water come waterfowl. Ducks arrive almost immediately upon establishment of the pond. Black ducks, wood ducks, and hooded mergansers seem to be most common on beaver flows. Mallards have increased significantly in numbers recently. Indeed, studies at the SUNY College of Environmental Science and Forestry summer campus on Cranberry Lake reveal that a modest amount of hybridization between mallards and black ducks has occurred locally. I occasionally see pairs of ducks, often with their broods, that I cannot clearly distinguish. I assume that these are hybrids between the two.

Both wood ducks and hooded mergansers use hollow tree cavities as nest sites. I have often wondered if there was an ample enough supply of snags for both species around every pond. The answer perhaps lies in the hollow hardwood snag lying in shallow water that I came upon one memorable spring day in the Cranberry Lake Wild Forest. Within the hollow was a mixed clutch of eggs with females of both species alternating incubating duties. I have since learned that studies done by SUNY ESF at Newcomb reveal this inter-species bonding to be not entirely uncommon.

The similarity of the two species seems to terminate with the nest site and habitat, however. The hooded merganser is a profligate fish-eater while the wood duck relies on plant life, including beechnuts, for food. This divergence in taste is why it is possible for them to coexist in the same habitat.

Great blue herons haunt the shores of beaver ponds, wading along in the shallows as they avidly seek an unwary frog or fish to spear for supper. Often their nest colonies are in the flooded trees that line beaver ponds. Even when their colonies are located away from the ponds, the bounteous prey available there draws them repeatedly to the sites.

I have vivid memories of removing a leghold trap from the foot of a great blue heron on the shores of a secluded beaver pond one frosty November morning. A friend, trapping for mink, had inadvertently caught the heron and requested my assistance in removing the trap and freeing the bird. My trepidation on viewing the long and lethal-looking spear that served as the heron's beak was considerable to say the least. So, too, was the immense satisfaction derived from successfully removing the trap! One doleful glance at us and the heron rose with difficulty then flew ponderously away.

The shores of beaver ponds are further enlivened by the frequent presence of the spotted sandpiper as it teeters along on spindly legs. It nests locally, but I have never discovered a nest site of this master of deception. The solitary sandpiper does not breed locally as far as we know, but I often encounter it around our beaver ponds. Its spring and autumn migrating times almost overlap so it is present a good part of the summer season. It teeters up and down as it walks along the shore, but whenever I dwell on this bird it is its sharp, distinctive call that I conjure up.

No call, however, excites me as much as that of the rolling rattle of the kingfisher as it dives from its tree perch into the pond to secure an unwary fish for supper. What that fish most often is has become the subject of much debate of late. Hard-line sportsmen claim the kingfisher takes only trout, while equally hard-line environmentalists insist only "coarse fish" appear on its menu. The answer probably lies somewhere in between, as both trout and "coarse fish" have apparently coexisted successfully with kingfishers since the waning of the last glacier some 10,000 years ago.

As the process of ecological succession proceeds onward, the beaver pond gradually evolves into a marsh. Usually this occurs after the disappearance of the beaver due to the decline of the woody vegetation that has sustained it. The marsh has its own distinctive wildlife and is an equally fascinating locale for the visit of a wildlife watcher.

As the dam is breached upon the beaver's disappearance, the pond slowly begins to recede. At first standing pools remain in some low-lying areas. Some of the frogs and turtles that have multiplied significantly in numbers with the pond's establishment still find a habitat here. Green frogs and bull frogs are especially attracted to beaver ponds and the green frog remains as long as pools do. So do painted turtles. I often see them basking on old beaver dams seeking sunlight in early spring. Leopard frogs and pickerel frogs remain in the marsh all summer, frantically hunting insects. This appears to occur even if the marsh is entirely without water.

Certain of the aquatic insects of the pond are still around in this stage. The mayfly, which as an aquatic nymph provided food for a host of fish, frogs, crayfish and even dragonfly nymphs, now takes wing toward dusk and begins its haunting mating flight over the marsh as it does over pond and brook. The flight of the dragonfly is also seen over the beaver marsh, more spectacular and less ephemeral than that of mayflies. But then the dragonfly is concerned with obtaining food as well as mating in its flight patterns!

When a luxuriant growth of sedges and blue joint grass, along with cattails, becomes established and still has occasional pools of water interspersed around it, conditions become optimum for muskrats. They feed heavily on the roots, tubers, and stems of marsh vegetation. Their lodges, which differ from those of the beaver in being composed primarily of non-woody materials, are often evident in the beaver marsh. At other times, the muskrats nest in bank dens. They are preyed on by mink, but I suspect the muskrats give a good account of themselves before succumbing. I have seen one turn and abruptly face a marsh harrier who sallied over its head. However, the strongest witness to their pugnacity that I have observed came about as follows.

It was early June, just before daybreak, on the shores of a backcountry beaver marsh. I had hiked the two miles to this spot while participating in the New York State Breeding Bird Census in 1983. While hiking through the marsh grass preparing to listen for the dawn chorus of breeding male songbirds, I noticed a movement in the vegetation quite near me. Being of a curious nature, especially where creatures of the wild are concerned, I went closer for a better look. At that, a muskrat (for such was the maker of the movement) lunged like a streak of lightning and delivered a vicious bite just under my knee. Fortunately I was wearing hip boots and, although the bite pierced the rubber, my skin was spared. Ever since I have never dared to question the fighting spirit of a muskrat!

The thick vegetation in the marsh is ideal for certain water birds. The loud "stake-pump" call of the common bittern can be heard emanating from all parts of the marsh. The long-legged bittern, thin as a reed himself, appears indistinguishable from the drab-colored grasses that ideally match its color. The marsh is also home to the common snipe. I listen entranced to its haunting, winnowing cry all through the month of May. The woodcock, too, is here on the edge of the marsh. Its distinctive nocturnal nasal "peent" and fluttering of wings during spring courting combine with the ethereal call of the snipe to make a thoughtful person reflect on things not of this realm during this season.

After dusk I regularly hear woodcocks on the more established beaver marshes as they probe the alders on the fringe for the plentiful supply of earthworms. The supply always seems adequate to fuel their nuptial endeavors.

Harriers are regularly seen patrolling slowly over the marsh, seeking meadow voles and such for their bill of fare. If the harrier is a venturesome sort, it might tackle a muskrat. Its dining successfully in the latter instance is not always certain, however. In either case, beaver marshes undoubtedly provide close to optimal habitat for the marsh harrier in the Adirondack Park.

Another raptor seen regularly around a beaver marsh is the red-tailed hawk. The muskrat is a regular part of its menu also, but meadow voles appear to be even more important. In my experience, red-tailed requires the most extensive beaver marshes for habitat and is absent from some of the smaller ones. I often see it on top of large snags on the marsh. Red-shouldered hawks, too, gravitate to the vicinity of beaver flows. They seem to prefer the beaver pond more than the marsh, but I see them on both. Occasionally, I hear both of these large raptors calling in close proximity to each other. In addition to the usual fare of small mammals, the red-shouldered hawk seems to utilize many more herptiles on its menu. I often watch them preying on a variety of frogs and small garter snakes. I once watched in fascination as a soaring red-shouldered suddenly dropped its prey—a toad, quite lifeless— back into the marsh. Since the hawk left the scene on my arrival, it remains an open question whether it would have retrieved the toad from had I not put in an appearance!

Broad-winged hawks frequently hunt on the fringes of the marsh, although their nests are usually far removed from here. They also appear to relish a variety of herptiles and, accordingly, leave their nests in small openings in the hardwoods so that they can easily hunt beaver flows and marshes in the vicinity.

The moose is undoubtedly the most majestic inhabitant of beaver ponds and marshes. Adirondack moose have indicated a preference for the vicinity of beaver flows and marshes over all other habitats. The food here includes the roots of water lilies and other aquatic vegetation as well as the succulent browse of willows and red osier dogwoods. The tough stems of marsh grass are also utilized upon occasion. In addition to these culinary attractions, moose find, in old beaver flows, merciful respite from the relentless attacks of legions of Adirondack biting flies.

As the marsh undergoes yet another transition by slowly evolving into a meadow, an entirely different wildlife community emerges and reveals itself. The flowering herbs sprinkled among the tall grass attract a slew of brilliant-hued butterflies as pollinators; they positively light up the meadow on a sunlit summer day. Many of those other flying jewels, the dragonflies and damselflies, remain from the pond; and a host of swallows, waxwings and others of their ilk, swoop and swerve after them in a valiant attempt at population control. All seems in vain, however, as the flowers inevitably get pollinated and there is a new crop of dragonflies the following year to take their turn harassing smaller flying insects. When the fireflies arrive to electrify the night with their sparkling points of light, we begin to realize what an enchanted place a beaver pond truly is!

Red-tailed hawk and marsh harrier sally over the meadow, but their intended prey is now more often woodchuck instead of muskrat. Meadow voles and meadow jumping mice constantly scurry among the grasses pursued by both coyotes and red fox. The coyote, especially, has to catch myriad of these small rodents to meet its nutritional needs. Coyotes dig dens on the banks of both beaver ponds and in meadows. These dens are often in evidence as the coyote frequently moves as the year progresses. Fox dens are more often on an elevated knoll back in the woods, but I also find them in beaver meadows that have begun to revert to brush. The remains of prey are littered liberally around the dens. An exciting spectacle I have often witnessed is the sight of a red fox carefully pouncing on an unsuspecting vole with all four paws, pinning it to the ground. After the fox has captured a few voles, it usually retreats into the adjoining woods.

I find the beaver meadow is not an especially favored feeding ground for the white-tailed deer. The tender browse of green leaves in the forest appears to be more to its preference. The dry areas of the beaver meadow are favorite locations for the beds of this, the Great South Woods' favorite ungulate, however. The flattened areas where deer have rested are prominent in beaver meadows until a mantle of white finally covers the ground.

In the days of not-too-distant yore, beaver meadows were the favorite haunt of another large cervid, the elk. Recent studies have shown that elk made substantial use of blue joint and other grasses that dominate these meadows. The elk originally existed in large numbers in the St. Lawrence Valley and wandered up the smaller river valleys into the Great South Woods.

As the beaver pond gradually evolves in stages through marsh to meadow, the forest fringing its shores also undergoes its own transformation. A clearing has emerged as a result of the beavers' cutting of all woody browse for distances of up to one hundred yards from the water's edge. This clearing then starts upon its own resolute process of succession, from flowers and herbs to brush and finally back to forest, barring, of course, the return of the beaver to begin things all over again!

The resultant increase in sunlight leads to a rapid proliferation of browse which attracts a variety of prey species such as voles and broods of ruffed grouse to the area. The latter are attracted by both the browse and the increased supply of insects. In summer, deer frequently come to the clearing, both for the increased amount of browse and for the relief that the waters of the pond affords from the biting flies. Deer positively seem to relish browsing on the beaver-cut hardwoods that sprout so profusely in the clearing.

With the increase in prey species also comes an increase in the corresponding predators. I often come upon signs of red fox in these clearings. Occasionally, I even see the red prince himself.

The opening in the canopy now existing around the pond and marsh leads to an increase in the wildflowers of forest openings and brushlands as well. Songbirds are quick to exploit this niche. I seldom visit the environs of a beaver wetland without hearing the plaintive melody of the white-throated sparrow. This cheery lyric, which the Canadians interpret as "oh sweet Canada," has become emblematic of the Great South Woods for me. Song sparrows, chestnut-sided warblers, yellowthroats, least flycatchers—their songs and calls have now become regular in the area. I find their melodies add pleasant variety and that they pleasingly complement the songs of the interior forest birds.

In addition, these open areas appear to furnish the ideal habitat for the establishment of the elegantly blossoming shrubs of the Great

South Woods. Whether the primary cause for their proliferation is the increase in sunshine or an increase in the moisture regime adjacent to the wetland, it is a fact that the best place to see Adirondack blossoms in their full glory is at these openings adjoining beaver flows. Shadbush and hobblebush seem to be especially favored here. A trip to any of the interior beaver ponds in the Five Ponds Wilderness Area during May will instantly confirm this. A little later, elderberry comes into bloom and adds its dramatic blossoms to the floral display. Often I find elderberry growing right on the beaver dam itself. The fragrance and the delightful wine made from the tart fruit give joy without compare!

As the process of ecological succession inevitably proceeds on its course, an upland forest will once again hold sway in the area. The brook will meander back into its channel again and the flora and fauna of pond, marsh, and meadow will be replaced by that of a typical Adirondack forest. How soon this occurs depends primarily on the length of stay of the beaver. Generally they will stay until their food supply is exhausted or until they are removed by predation or trapping. I know beaver impoundments where beaver are still present and the flowage basically intact after forty years! Normally, beaver impoundments are transitory in nature and exist in an ever-fluctuating pattern across the landscape, but a few appear to have become at least semi-permanent. In the cases I have seen, topography seems to be the main causative factor. The inlet ponds above Big Otter Pond in the Five Ponds Wilderness and the Scuttle Hole Chain of ponds in the Aldrich Pond Wild Forest readily spring to mind.

I know of dams up to five hundred feet in length that have created flowages up to fifty acres in extent. These megadams do not necessarily create the longest-lasting pond, although the Scuttle Hole Chain appears to fit into this category. The two inlet dams to Big Otter are relatively short dams strategically placed in a narrow chasm between solid bedrock. Both of these appear to have withstood the test of time.

Ultimately, in the normal course of events, there will come a time when the typical beaver flowage must start its slow progression back to forest, utilizing all the intermediary stages on the way. The beaver have departed and the age-old cycle begins anew! Thus a provision is made for a multitude of varied habitats and the resultant vital enhancement of biodiversity in the forests of the Great South Woods.

VI

SIGHTS IN THE FOREST

Photo courtesy of Betsy Tisdale

Jamestown Falls, Raquette River

Landforms and artifacts are scattered throughout the rivers, ponds, and pinnacles of the Great South Woods. They go right to the very recesses of the forest. Most are of the natural order and have lain on the landscape since the melting of the ice some 10,000 years ago. A few are man-made and have existed in the forest since the advent of European settlement. All now blend deftly into the local terrain and appear to truly be an indelible part of the landscape.

ESKERS and BOGS

The "road through the bog" is the Gaelic translation of the word "esker." Could anything be more fitting since eskers seem inevitably to wind their way through a mixture of ponds and peatlands? In some local instances eskers have actually been the base for roads; Massawepie Lake Road comes readily to mind.

Eskers reach their crowning glory in the Great South Woods. The area hosts the most splendid eskers in the state of New York and perhaps the entire Northeast. Almost all at some point bisect a peatland or else encircle its perimeter. Peatlands, or bogs, also approach the ultimate in size and number in the Great South Woods. They are exceeded only by certain bogs in northern and central Maine. The two are invariably entwined in the Great South Woods and it is as such that I treat them.

Eskers came into being upon the melting of the glacial ice and the deposition of long, sandy serpentine ridges that were the residue of streams running inside that ice. All eskers are, hence, quite sandy or gravelly.

A plethora of mixed conifers appears to grow on top of these sandy ridges. There is an occasional red maple or yellow birch, but very rarely beech and almost never sugar maple.

Some of the eskers have their length in scores of miles. They occasionally taper off to ground level and then re-emerge a distance away to continue their winding path through the landscape. Large eskers appear to absorb smaller ones, much in the manner of small creeks being absorbed into larger streams. Often these smaller eskers also have peatlands at their feet.

The Five Ponds Esker is perhaps the best known of all. Famous for its virgin conifer stands, it lies mainly in an area that is among the most remote in the state. Its shining jewels are the towering stands of white pine and red spruce that adorn its crest for much of the route. One hiking trail, the Sand Lake Trail, penetrates the area and a glimpse of the virgin timber can be had along its way. Diminished by the microburst of 1995 and other windstorms, it is truly still an impressive sight. There is an osprey nest on this esker and I have often been treated to the spectacle of this hawk-eagle diving into one of the tiny Five Ponds for a meal of fish. Bear paths are a frequent sight and twice I have come upon coyote dens dug into the side of the esker.

The Cranberry Lake Esker is also well known. There is some old-growth timber here, especially the mammoth white pine in the vicinity of Nick's Pond. A portion of this esker is used for the canoe carry between the Bog River and the Oswegatchie River; this is a good place to become acquainted with the esker. The Six Mile Creek Trail also travels on it for part of its route. Deer trails commonly lace the top of the esker. As there is little in the way of food for deer on top, I can only surmise that it is the sense of security offered by the ridge itself that is the main attraction here.

The third large esker that is well known in the region is the Massawepie Esker. This imposing ridge supports a town road for at least four miles. The road winds its merry way with a series of enchanting kettle ponds lining it on the east. On the west lies sprawling Massawepie Lake with the huge Massawepie Bog just beyond it.

In addition to towering white pine and hemlock, Massawepie Esker possesses a special gem unique to itself. That is the impressive stand of the rarely seen red pine that graces its flanks and tops. Trailing arbutus, twin flower, and pipsissewa add their showy and uncommon blossoms to the floral display on the floor of the forest.

An osprey nest is also present in the top of a white pine on the esker. In addition a glacial tarn, Pine Pond, is nestled between the folds of the esker. Massawepie Lake adds lake trout and the endangered lake whitefish to the splendor of the local fauna.

A bog would seem much diminished in my eyes without an esker to light the path over it. Diminished, too, would be the Great South Woods without the presence of these "paths" traversing portions of it!

The peatlands themselves have a definite aura of the primeval about them. Low-lying and misty, they have an assemblage of plant life that is generally quite primitive in nature. They are cool, nutrient-poor and characterized usually by impeded drainage and soil acid. This translates to difficult growing conditions that most plants are incompatible with. The ones that do thrive here tend to be quite unusual and, in addition, often attain their allotment of nutrients in a most unorthodox fashion. For instance, two mainstays of bog flora, the pitcher plant and the sundew, acquire their nutrients by devouring insects!

The heath family is particularly well-represented in peatlands. Members include the gorgeous blooms of sheep laurel and bog laurel as well as more prosaic ones such as Labrador tea, bog rosemary, and andromeda. Prosaic in blossoms, perhaps, but certainly not in their names!

Sphagnum moss is the underlying firmament of the bog. The partially decayed remains of previous vegetation, it also sprawls over the surface of the peatlands and adds to both its acidity and wetness. There are several different species in the peatlands of the Great South Woods. One of them is a sharp reddish color and supplies a touch of scarlet throughout the year.

Peatlands are of two general types—bogs and fens. Fens are somewhat richer in nutrients and less acidic than bogs. Many of our peatlands exhibit characteristics of both.

In addition to the larger peatlands discussed here, there are scores of tiny peatlands scattered across the terrain like dimples in the folds of the forest.

Massawepie Mire is the largest open peatland in the Adirondacks. Massawepie, actually a fen, is pierced by the old Grass River Railroad bed, now graveled as a roadway. Although the bog is owned privately, the railroad bed is owned by New York State and provides excellent access to the area.

Sedges are as much in abundance in Massawepie as is sphagnum moss. This is one of the reasons for classifying it as a fen. However, the most outstanding facet of Massawepie from any criteria is the fabulous birdlife in its environs. Many of these avian specialties are absent elsewhere in New York. Spruce grouse leads the list here. This enormous peatland complex probably possesses the largest population of this endangered species in the entire state. I often observe eagles soaring overhead and feel it is a distinct possibility bald eagles and perhaps even golden eagles have a nest in the immediate vicinity.

It is, however, with the breeding boreal birds that avian splendor reaches its full zenith. Over a score of palm warblers were recently found breeding here. Before this, only one or two pairs were known to breed in New York. These were at Spring Pond Bog, which is on the periphery of the Great South Woods and owned by the Nature Conservancy. White-winged crossbills, boreal chickadee, and Lincoln's sparrow all breed regularly at Massawepie and rarely elsewhere in the state.

Sevey's Bog is also quite large, over 300 acres in extent. Formerly open to the public under a Fish and Wildlife Agreement Act with the DEC, the bog is now posted and off limits to the public.

I heard my first calling of the spruce grouse here, identified for me by Dale Garner of SUNY ESF while we were at the bog looking for signs of moose. I had previously heard the call for a number of years, but was unable to identify it. It pays to have friends!

Canada jays are also present at Sevey's Bog, as is the rusty blackbird among other boreal specialties. Deer trails lace the surface of the peatland; most deer are traveling through because few of the flora here provide ample enough nutrients to interest a deer. Some in the peatland even have chemicals in their leaves to discourage browsing by herbivores.

Streeter Bog is rather unknown but this is changing slowly mainly due to bird-finding expeditions to its environs. I never fail to come here in season without hearing the song of the ruby-crowned kinglet or the plaintive call of the yellow-bellied flycatcher. Canada jays flock from the bog to be fed at local hunting camps come November. When I conjure up images of Streeter Bog it is the gorgeous bloom of the rose pogonia that comes most readily to mind. This wild orchid seems everywhere to flaunt its delicate blossoms above the bog mat in early July.

These peatlands bestow an additional element of wonder and mystery to the Great South Woods. Without their allure a vital part of the forest fabric would be absent.

GLACIAL ERRATICS

Often while wandering deep in the forest in an unfamiliar area I would sight in the distance what I'd first take to be a modest-sized house. Upon cessation of my incredulity at the presence in the middle of nowhere of a major emblem of mankind, the truth of the matter gradually unfolded. These were not edifices left by man but rather mementos left by the last Ice Age. Upon melting, glaciers delivered assorted bedrock gathered from farther north entirely in the position they were in when the melting occurred. Hence the occurrence of "glacial erratics"—huge boulders which are frequently found in the Great South Woods of today.

The size of some of these glacial boulders is truly awesome. Two in particular are located on the Dead Creek Flow Trail and on the Burntbridge Pond Trail. In both cases they are immediately adjacent to the trail itself and make a considerable impression on hikers new to the area.

Although originating in points north, the rock material of the erratics usually conforms to the underlying bedrock of the area. In our area this is mostly the pinkish granitic gneiss that is so pleasing to the eye. This similarity to the underlying bedrock is mostly because the glacial erratic has usually been transported in miles measured by the dozens rather than the hundreds.

The boulders harbor a unique floral assemblage on their tops after enough moss has accumulated to form a substrate for the germination of seeds. Spruce, yellow birch, and hemlock can be seen growing blissfully on their tops. On the more modest-sized erratics, occasional trees may attain an impressive size as their roots follow the cushion of moss down the sides of the rock to find succor in the soil of the forest floor! Rock polypody is an attractive woodland fern that invariably seems to grow on the tops of the boulders along with the trees and moss.

Recent studies at the SUNY ESF campus at Newcomb have uncovered the fact that the ferns are mainly restricted to the tops of boulders because of the strong appeal they have for browsing deer. This is one of the few places in the forest where they are inaccessible to white-tailed deer!

Countless miles of trekking and tracking in the Great South Woods have revealed to me a most interesting connection between glacial erratics and bobcat. It appears these striking felines have an overwhelming fascination for the tops of even the largest glacial boulders. From these pedestals they sit for hours staring through the dark of the forest unfurled before them. They no doubt are seeking prey, but there is, I believe, more to it than that. To know the fullness of that "more to it," watch a house cat on a windowsill as it stares in rapture for hours at matters transpiring outside!

To me these glacial boulders are another element giving definition to the very nature of the Great South Woods.

CASCADES

Where running water winding on its way to the mighty St. Lawrence makes an abrupt, often dramatic, descent from a higher to a lower level: such a description defines a cascade in the Great South Woods. The sudden drop is due primarily to the differences in the hardness of the underlying bedrock and consequently to the resulting differences in resistance to the abrasive and erosional effects of the swiftly flowing water. Since the demise of the last glacier this has resulted in considerable differences in the level in the bedrock over which the water is running.

As the Great South Woods is located to a large degree in the area where running water takes its leave of the Adirondack plateau and commences its descent to the St. Lawrence, cascades are a feature of the local landscape. Several prominent cascades are discussed in the chapter on the "Bob Marshall Wilderness." Many other cascades are scattered throughout the forest. A few of the more notable are discussed here. They range from rather modest descents to truly dramatic plunges that border on the spectacular. The sylvan surroundings of their locales enhance the image they leave with seekers of the wonderful.

LAMPSON FALLS

This is a truly awesome cataract that has a total descent of some seventy feet and a width that closely corresponds. Spectacular in every respect, it would have a string of strip development around it were it not in such a remote location.

Fortunately, Lampson Falls was preserved for posterity mainly through the efforts of one man, Paul Jamieson of Canton. Paul, retired English professor at St. Lawrence University and canoe raconteur par excellence, personally escorted the commissioner of the DEC to the scene and prevailed upon him to protect the falls by purchasing it for inclusion in the Forest Preserve. As a result it is available for all to enjoy today.

Lampson Falls receives heavy use at certain times of the year. Still, at other times, solitude can be had even at this spectacular location, just you and the cedar waxwings swooping insects out of the air as the foam from the cascading water drifts upwards as a fine mist. It is at times like this that the realization takes place that this certainly is a grand time to be on the South Branch of the Grass River!

HARPER FALLS

Where the wild butternut grows, on the North Branch of the Grass River, just above its confluence with the South Branch: such would describe the location of Harper Falls.

A stunning plunge of nearly seventy feet, Harper rivals Lampson Falls in height. Because the width of its drop is far narrower than the descent, it does not quite match Lampson in overall splendor. Still it is spectacular in its own fashion and a definite feast for eyes that search for beauty to behold.

As at Lampson, there are remnants of old foundations near the falls. Could this bear testimony to another nineteenth century attempt to harness the raw power in the falls for industrial purposes?

Basswood and poison ivy put in rare appearances along the river here. They add a little floral diversity to augment the regular boreal vegetation that otherwise prevails.

Harper Falls was purchased around a decade and a half ago from a private hunting club, the 400 Club. The number referred to the purported acreage in the tract. Upon purchase by New York State, an official survey determined that the true acreage was actually in excess of six hundred. The state had therefore to pay that corresponding amount! No matter, the joy rendered to the public from acquiring Harper Falls made the added expenditure well worth it.

JAMESTOWN and MOODY FALLS

These two falls are separated from each other by less than a mile on the Raquette River. They are both quite impressive, more in their width than their actual drop, which is only moderate. The sheer ruggedness of the river and the beauty of the surrounding forest more than compensate for this modesty in total descent.

Jamestown takes its name from a club here at the interface of the Forest Preserve and private land. Moody commemorates a father and son lumberjack duo who, in a moment of errant bravado, attempted to run the falls on a dark, stormy night. They failed in their attempt, but in so doing contributed their names to the legacy of the Great South Woods.

Jamestown Falls has the river backed up almost to its foot by the dam at Carry Falls Reservoir. Walleye fishing is often a rewarding pastime here. Moody Falls is best defined by the imposing white pine monarchs on its bank and the blueberry bushes that proliferate on the ledges overlooking the falls.

The two bespeak a subtle wonder and sparkle that is so much in evidence in the Great South Woods.

GREENWOOD FALLS

This is a cataract of a different nature, so to speak. It lies just outside the Adirondack Park, for one, in the Greenwood Creek State Forest. For another, much of the underlying bedrock is calcerous. This translates into the presence of sweeter soil and hence some of the more startling spring blossoms in the vicinity of the falls. Bloodroot and hepatica are regularly seen, along with an occasional wild ginger.

The marble also accounts for fissures and caves nearby, which have served to entice generations of bobcats to its environs. I regularly track them here in the snows of winter.

A nature trail constructed by the St. Lawrence County Youth Conservation Corps leads through an attractive red pine plantation on the banks of Greenwood Creek. The pines replaced the hay fields of the Depression era, according to John Sykes, whose house I purchased in the early 1970s. A charming picnic area is located under the pines: all the more reason to visit Greenwood Falls.

Some of the most spectacular waterfalls of all became available to the general public in the summer of 2000. They lie along the South Branch of the Grass River in the parcel that is in the process of being transferred from the Champion Paper Company to the state of New York. To my way of thinking, it was a day of bliss when these river jewels were finally opened for all to enjoy.

THE PLAINS

The Plains is completely unique to the Great South Woods. Classified as a boreal heath by the New York Natural Heritage Group, the Plains stands virtually alone as an extensive treeless area in an otherwise heavily wooded landscape.

The Plains occupies the wide valley floor between Three Mile Mountain and Round Top Mountain. It is drained by Glasby Creek, which empties into the Oswegatchie River shortly after leaving the Plains. The soils are sandy and subject to drought in late summer. Come spring, however, they are usually flooded with the heavy snow melt of winter. This is one of the factors impeding the general growth of trees. Another is probably the dense growth of spirea which hinders both seed germination and then successful early growth.

Perhaps the main factor retarding tree regeneration, however, is the fact that the Plains appears to be a massive frost pocket. When Ray Curran of the APA did his thesis on the vegetation of the Plains, he discovered there was a hard frost in every month of the summer he was there. In this the Plains is somewhat similar to the many kettle holes in the Great South Woods. Most support ponds or a bog in their depressions, but few have progressed to the stage of supporting herbs and shrubs.

Some trees are encroaching on the sandy soils of the Plains, black cherry, tamarack, and black spruce mainly. The cherry branches have been disemboweled by bears climbing for fruit; the tamarack have many skeletons still standing as a result of being devastated by an infestation of larch sawfly; and the spruce appears to regenerate mainly by layering. Otherwise a thick cover of blueberry, black chokeberry, and selected grasses predominates, along with the spirea or meadowsweet previously mentioned.

Early settlers to the area found the Plains already in existence. They cut wild hay here and transported it to the settled portions of the town of Fine to feed their livestock. Cornelius Carter, a turn-of-the-century hermit and poet, utilized the Plains to pasture his sheep. A famous spring that allayed the thirst of innumerable woodsmen graced the edge of the Plains. Called the "boiling spring," it was a landmark of note for years.

Alas, the spring is no more. But the Plains still is, bringing with it a sense of wonder and uniqueness to the Great South Woods.

FIRE TOWERS

They stood like beacons in the distance, mute witness to an era that has passed. That era was the time when fire detection was conducted primarily from towers placed upon the tops of mountains. That technique has now been supplanted almost entirely by surveillance from helicopter flights conducted at regular intervals. This has made most fire towers obsolete.

The majority of them have been dismantled. One, on Mount Arab, remains standing, but unused. Its condition slowly deteriorates as it stands exposed to the elements. The fire observer's cabin beneath it is succumbing to the ravages of marauding porcupines and mindless human vandals. A restoration effort led by a local group with the support of the Adirondack Mountain Club and the DEC may result in their being repaired and opened again to the public for educational purposes.

As related in another previous chapter, the DEC observer for decades here went by the name of "Woody." Woody had a penchant for regaling one with anecdotes after a climb to share the tower with him. These tales were always interesting and, as far as I can determine, always accurate. Over the years he experienced several encounters with black bears; these he related in a manner made more compelling by the ambiance of the setting.

Two of the peaks named after felines in the Great South Woods also once had fire towers gracing their crests. The two are Cat Mountain, deep in the Five Ponds Wilderness, and Catamount Mountain, overlooking Carry Falls Reservoir. All that remains of the towers today in both places are the concrete foundations.

From 1911 until the Depression, Cat Mountain was manned by John Janack, who raised a large brood of children at the site. The family dwelling was actually on Dead Creek Flow, at the spot where Janack's lean-to is located today.

The fire observer on Catamount Mountain was for many years Miles McCarthy of Colton, New York. Catamount has some gnarled old apple trees on its top, as well as at the base of the fire tower and the observer's cabin. Cat Mountain is also home to a few apple trees on its upper slope that are slowly withering towards oblivion.

There were also fire towers on Moosehead Mountain and Tooley Pond Mountain in our area. Tooley Pond Mountain opened for use by the general public in the summer of 2000 as part of the Champion-New York State land transfer.

I recall a series of scintillating seconds a decade ago on top of St. Regis Mountain. An electrical storm passed over Mount Arab and the fire observer there relayed a warning to the observer in the tower on St. Regis Mountain. A sense of tense anxiety tinged with excitement, a rapid descent from the tower and then the exhilaration of safety attained. Nothing could better dramatize the power of the elements and the sense of the primeval that is still so much a part of the Great South Woods!

OLD RAILROAD BEDS

Today they wind through the forest in the most unlikely places, another memento of a past era in the Great South Woods. These are the beds of the railroads that were once used to transport the felled virgin timber to the mills. The old beds, now utilized as hiking or snowmobile trails, have outlasted the lumberjacks, trains, and track of bygone days.

Some of the most intensively used trails in our area are underlain by these railroad beds. Foremost among these are the beds of the old Rich Lumber Company, which played such a prominent part in the founding of the hamlet of Wanakena. The company constructed an intricate series of interconnecting lines that enabled them to move timber from the far-flung reaches of their expansive domain to mills in the hamlet and at Newton Falls. These are the bases, today, for the High Falls Truck Trail and the neighboring Dead Creek Flow Trail. Their mostly level grades are in stark contrast to the normal undulating pattern made by other trails in this region.

The Mecca Lumber Company played the same role in the founding of the hamlet of Kalurah as the Rich Lumber Company did in Wanakena. A mill was established here and the virgin forest was decimated using logging railroads to transport the raw trees to the mill. The trail through the Forest Preserve to Round Lake proceeds on a remnant of these old railroad beds. The entrancing name for the hamlet originated from a rather prosaic source: it was named after the Masonic lodge in Binghamton, New York!

Aldrich was also once a thriving logging hamlet. Two churches and a school, in addition to the mill, flourished where now only rustic hunting camps and a few residences remain. The logs were extracted from the forest almost exclusively by railroad. The DEC truck road from Aldrich to Streeter Lake proceeds on the bed of the mainline. Other trails go over old railroad beds to the Middle Branch of the Oswegatchie River, where a "jackworks" or log boom was located near the intersection of the river and Pins Creek. In some places these trails reveal dramatically the outline of the old railroad. In a few others, remains of the old railroad ties are clear.

The Grass River Railroad linking the hamlets of Cranberry Lake and Conifer was primarily a logging railroad. The first several miles of the Burntbridge Pond Trail uses a spur of this line in winding its way through the forest. Most of the mainline itself is today a graveled road that proceeds for miles through Massawepie Bog and the adjacent Grass River Flow. Owned now by New York State, it is open to the public for hiking and skiing and is in fact not only the best, but the only way to become acquainted with the many wonders of this dramatic peatland.

These old railroad beds convey a touch of the past every bit as much as the forest trails today built on their foundation now convey travelers to points of destination in the Great South Woods. They now move lovers of the forest as the railroads once moved the parts of that forest in the days of yore!

Near Sevey's Corners, St. Lawrence County

Photo by Gerry Lemmo

Timberwolf

Photo by Gerry Lemmo

Bobcat

Photo by Gerry Lemmo

Marten

Photo courtesy of Duncan Cutter

Lampson Falls

Photo courtesy of Duncan Cutter

St. Regis Mountain from St. Regis Pond

Nine-point buck

Fire Tower on Azure Mountain

Greenwood Creek Falls

Photo by Gerry Lemmo

Bald Eagle

Photo by Gerry Lemmo

Black Bear

Photo by Gerry Lemmo

Coyote

Photo by Gerry Lemmo

Wild Turkey

VII

THE RIVERS

Photo courtesy of Duncan Cutter

Bog River

The moving waters that carry away the abundant precipitation of the Great South Woods have been likened to the arterial veins that give definition to the human anatomy. They not only delineate the various watersheds, but in many instances serve to define quite diverse elements of local flora and fauna. Early man, too, utilized many of these moving waters as aquatic highways, paddling and portaging across the rugged topography while traversing the area.

The rivers described here all flow north into the St. Lawrence. Indeed, three of them—Raquette, Grass, and St. Regis—flow into this majestic river, first seen by Europeans on the feast day of Saint Lawrence, within a distance of seven miles of each other.

The portions of these rivers I know most intimately are mainly in the Forest Preserve, although stretches along most of them still remain in private hands. If one word can describe the essence of these rivers, it would be wildness, of terrain and spirit. My familiarity with them began with canoeing, fishing, hunting (in a few instances), and wildlife viewing along the stretches open to the public.

Adirondack rivers are, in effect, classic examples of what are called ecotones, a merger of two quite distinct habitats. The wildlife of both habitats is present, as well as the unique wildlife that favors the ecotone itself. The merger of forest, opening, and water is perhaps the most productive of wildlife in the entire park. Rivers additionally furnish the soils of the adjacent shores with a higher pH than normally present, due to their well-oxygenated waters. This occasionally leads to the presence of certain species of flora usually restricted to areas of less overall soil acidity. Purple-fringed orchid, yellow lady slipper, and white trillium spring readily to mind.

An inescapable historical fact in connection with rivers has been a universal propensity of humankind to erect dams across them, thereby instantly creating an entirely different atmosphere and wildlife habitat. The dams were originally erected as "log booms" to hold felled timber until it could be transported farther downstream to the mill. Examples are the several jackworks constructed in the vicinity of Aldrich on both the Little River and the Middle Branch of the Oswegatchie. Later the dams were built to furnish general power for industrial activities: the two Bog River dams and the numerous dams erected on the Raquette River below Tupper Lake in connection with hydro-electric activities.

That so much in the way of free-running rivers still survives today in the Great South Woods attests both to a miracle of a minor nature as well as to the tenacity and vigilance of many early conservationists who struggled against the creation of major dam projects earlier in the century.

EAST BRANCH OSWEGATCHIE

By most parameters, perhaps the premier Adirondack wilderness river is the East Branch of the Oswegatchie between Inlet, two miles above where the river enters Cranberry Lake, and Beaver Dam, approximately six miles above High Falls. Located entirely within the Five Ponds Wilderness Area, the stretch is canoeable for its total length with the only impediments being a few minor rapids and the imposing cascade of High Falls. A trek by canoe here is a veritable paddle into the past, a glimpse of what most Adirondack rivers were like in the last century. The boreal landscape of tamarack, pine, and spruce prevailing along most of the stretch is more reminiscent of an Alaskan river than of the "Lower 48."

Certain memories of this river are etched indelibly in my mind. They vary across a wide spectrum, from the sight of yellow-rumped warblers and cedar waxwings frantically "hawking" a newly emergent mayfly hatch just off the water, to that of a frightened white-tailed doe swimming across the river with an aura of terror. I had to swerve the canoe to avoid hitting her. She clambered on shore and into the adjoining forest; I never did catch the identity of her pursuers. On several occasions I have also observed both porcupine and raccoon swimming across, but perhaps the memory that I recall most readily is one that I was not privileged to witness: two local DEC forest rangers were fortunate enough to have a moose cow and calf swim in front of their canoe in the early 1980s. They relayed the sighting to me and, human nature being what it is, I feel I saw it also.

From its start in the vicinity of Beaver Dam as a confluence of several small steams to the point where it enters Cranberry Lake on the Inlet Flow, the Oswegatchie reveals one delight after another. It widens considerably where the Robinson River makes its junction with it three miles above High Falls. As wide as the Oswegatchie at this point, this remote setting is as close as the Robinson River ever gets to civilization. I never pass the junction without pondering on Sliding Rock Falls, nestled six miles upstream in as primitive a setting as can be found in New York State. The downed aircraft that lay immersed for two decades in a beaver meadow adjacent to the river until being discovered by a trout fisherman, also never fails to come to mind.

Next comes the old-growth timber at Pine Ridge, a mile or so downriver from the meeting of the Oswegatchie and Robinson Rivers. Much of the virgin timber was decimated by the hurricane of 1950, but the venerable white pine Goliaths remaining are still quite impressive. Camp Johnny, a hallowed Adirondack camp on the river below the ridge, has many personal memories. The one springing most easily to mind is of a deer hunting expedition on which we camped here for a week in 1980. My partner and I had hung a magnificent eight-point buck just before retiring to our tent for the evening. Upon awakening at the crack of dawn, my partner excitedly pointed to the buck, which was quivering wildly as if it were still alive. Before we could verbally attest to a miracle, the mystery was solved by the exit of four Canada jays from inside the cadaver. They were having themselves quite a glorious dine-in!

High Falls, the hub of the wilderness with its lean-tos and connecting trails from Wanakena, is next encountered a few miles downstream. Dining at a campfire here in the evening often produces a delicious visual treat, the appearance of the elegantly attired woodland jumping mouse hopping all over the area in an attempt to filch food from the unwary. Although these handsome nocturnal creatures are abundant throughout the Adirondacks, the lean-tos at High Falls are the only place I have witnessed this activity of theirs.

The lean-tos are beloved of bears also. As often as not, one will amble over in a nighttime quest for quick food. Occasionally such a visit can be made in an alarming fashion. Such an occurrence happened the night I elected to sleep in a pup tent in order to protect myself from the ferocity of the mosquitoes and punkies. Around 3 A.M., a visiting bear actually attempted to flip me over as I lay in the tent. I awoke in a hurry and emitted a mighty yell of inquiry as to what was happening. Upon hearing the yell the bear exited the scene promptly and loudly. Afterwards I deduced two things from this incident: a) the bear possibly understood English, b) even more possible, my measure of luck was considerable that evening.

Downstream from High Falls it is only another few miles to a bit of the famous "plains" lying astride the river. At this point Glasby Creek empties its waters into the Oswegatchie.

The site of the bridge at Cage Lake Spring Hole is next. Now relegated to oblivion, the foot bridge was formerly part of the Five Ponds-Cage Lake loop hike. From what seems time immemorial there has been an osprey nest in the vicinity of Cage Lake Spring Hole, although more often than not the osprey will be found fishing for trout at one of the Five Ponds themselves rather than in the immediate vicinity of the river. This is as far upriver as any party I've been with has taken a brown trout; normally this tasty alien will not travel so far.

Griffin Rapids and its lean-tos come next, approximately two miles downriver from Cage Lake Spring Hole. The old-growth hardwoods lie, for the most part, beyond the river, since the wood in the immediate vicinity has been subject to heavy use by campers over the decades.

High Rock is the final spectacular landmark, just four miles above the canoe put-in at Inlet Landing. High Rock is a prominent glacial rock cliff with an expansive marsh lying at its base. The marsh, actually a wide floodplain of the Oswegatchie, encompasses several hun-.dred acres of swamp and wetland through which the river winds its way in a serpentine fashion, almost inscribing a perfect figure eight upon the landscape. The prevailing vegetation of alder and blue joint grass is the background for the haunting, otherworldly mating cry of the common snipe emanating from the May mists at dusk. Once heard, particularly in a setting such as this, its memory will be long retained!

Sightings of species not normally associated with such a boreal habitat can also be seen here. I think of the bobolink, calling from the drier part of the marsh all through June, finding here a substitute for the hay fields which in other parts of the state vie for its attention. That avian emblem of New York State, the bluebird, is present here also. It finds in the many dead hollow stubs at the edge of the marsh a ready substitute for the bird houses and orchard trees it uses in other areas.

Looming over this wide expanse of marsh is High Rock itself, and on top of it another traditional Adirondack campsite, which may also be reached by a rough trail from Wanakena. A singularly dramatic occurrence took place here while I was standing on the large protruding rock promontory overlooking the marsh. I pointed out to a companion what I took to be a large snag off by itself in the middle of the marsh. To my astonishment, but not that of my sharp-eyed companion, the snag suddenly moved and the most massive bear I've ever seen stood up on its forelegs and peered intently towards us. To the startled duo on the rock outcrop, his size appeared to be on a par with one of the legendary Alaskan brown bears depicted so often on screen. A twin at least! "Think of that!" exclaimed my companion. I often do!

The fabled Oswegatchie spring holes, legendary for producing brook trout upon demand, occur all along the river at points where auxiliary streams and brooks empty into it. The quality of the fishing here has diminished somewhat due, primarily, to the tendency of beavers to erect dams right at the point where the streams meet the river. This warms the water past the point where brook trout find it to their liking. Still, there are certain hallowed times where the fishing can be almost as productive as in days of yore. A little study of the area and a lot of luck are all that are needed!

LITTLE RIVER

The Little River arises near Heath Pond in wetlands only a short distance from the East Branch of the Oswegatchie. It flows about fifteen miles, making a sharp fishhook-shaped course before ultimately merging its waters with those of the Oswegatchie's east branch below the hamlet of Oswegatchie.

I am most familiar with the six-mile stretch of river between Star Lake and the hamlet of Aldrich. The river in this stretch lies almost wholly within the Forest Preserve and may be canoed with one carry around a waterfall a mile below Star Lake.

A dam, at the mill site in the hamlet of Aldrich during its lumbering heyday, created an extensive body of water called Aldrich Pond on the topo map. The demise of the dam left a sprawling floodplain for approximately two miles upriver. To canoe here in the spring, with the songs of breeding bird life in full chorus from every direction, is a singular delight. Sparrows galore—swamp, song, white-throated—plus yellow warblers and northern yellowthroats interspersed with marsh wrens and red-winged blackbirds; their melody rings cheerily and incessantly from out of the alders and marsh grass lining the floodplain. The floodplain setting with its abundant bird life makes the location seem less boreal than neighboring habitats.

In contrast to the bird life, which is at its height in the spring, August is the time of year when the river's best floral display comes to the fore. The red blossoms of the cardinal flower merge with the deep blue of narrow gentian, as both complement the off-purple of joe-pye weed and swamp milkweed to constantly line the route of the river. In July, elderberry and angelica were most prominent in bloom, with a corresponding complement of gorgeous fritillary butterflies pollinating them the length of the floodplain. Exposed sandbars are everywhere along this stretch, with the tracks of coyotes almost always registered in their cool mud. What accounts for this seeming fascination of canid with sand and flowing water? Surely the coyote comes here to drink, but is this the sole reason? I think not, especially considering the fact that the tracks reveal that the coyotes often seem to be merely prancing around aimlessly!

Above the confluence with Mud Creek, the floodplain disappears and high, wooded banks become the order of the day. The setting, approximately two miles above the juncture of river and creek, was the site of a finding most wondrous: a pair of elk antlers lying in a patch of alders alongside the river. The antlers were discovered by the owners of one of the hunting camps at Aldrich. What could possibly account for their presence in these remote reaches? All one can do is speculate. I see two possibilities: a) a bull elk met his demise here, b) someone has played a rather elaborate hoax for reasons known only to themselves.

Below Aldrich, the Little River tumbles four miles or so in a series of chilling cascades and cataracts to its meeting with the East Branch of the Oswegatchie. This stretch is occasionally run in spring by a most intrepid group of local paddlers. To do so successfully requires being the recipient of incredibly good fortune or alternately to possess adequate casualty insurance and be in the state of grace.

MIDDLE BRANCH OSWEGATCHIE

From its origins as the outlet of Walker Lake deep in the Five Ponds Wilderness, to its confluence with the West Branch of the Oswegatchie near the hamlet of Harrisville, the Middle Branch traverses as wild a section of forest land as it is possible for a river to flow through. Indeed the first score or more of miles are entirely in the Forest Preserve, a record rivaling that of its more famous sister, the East Branch.

This similarity to the East Branch extends to other areas also. Not the least of these is the presence along the Middle Branch of a large, sprawling wetland, Alder Bed Flow, which resembles, in a most uncanny manner, High Rock Marsh on the East Branch of the Oswegatchie. Spruce-fir plats line the Middle Branch for lengthy distances; in some places they take on the appearance of a savanna with large open areas of blue joint and other grasses interspersed among the trees. As on the East Branch, these conifer forests lining the river provide winter concentration areas for large numbers of white-tailed deer. The only thing missing on the Middle Branch is the presence of an occasional old-growth white pine looming over the general forest canopy beneath it.

I seem to encounter more mink here than along the other rivers. One ever-to-be-treasured moment was when one exited from the water and scurried between my legs on its way to plunging back into the water some thirty feet away. Swim away it did, not quite as rapidly as otter, which I have seen swim right through a beaver dam, seemingly without slowing down, but still swiftly enough to do justice to an Olympic swimmer.

The era of lumbering before state acquisition has left a longer-lasting legacy on the Middle Branch than on the East Branch of the Oswegatchie. One location on the river is widely known locally as the "jackworks." It is approximately three miles south of Streeter Lake, where a large "log boom" was erected across the river to impound its water in conjunction with the intensive lumbering around 1900. Some slim remnants remain at the site today. The spot has also for six decades been the cherished hunting domain of the McAdam family, who have maintained a temporary, rustic camp here while acquiring a slew of lasting memories. Therein lies a tale!

In a classic rendition of those paradoxes that seem to present themselves perennially in the Great South Woods, a unique, resource-based lifestyle was almost obliterated in a noble effort to protect and preserve the environment and resources which were part of that lifestyle! The Middle Branch had been officially declared a "wild river" and as such there could be no infringements of any human nature within three hundred feet of its banks. The locale of the McAdams' campsite and their method of transportation to reach it intruded on the scene, at least in a bureaucratic sense. I stress the latter because, from a natural point of view, the setting was as pristine as ever after usage by the McAdams family.

Initially the bureaucracy was rigid and inflexible: the McAdams would have to go! This raised quite a furor locally and public hearings were convened in response to the outcry. A compromise was reached thanks to the timely intervention of DEC Region 6 director Tom Brown, and the reasonableness of the APA on the issue. The resulting agreement both eminently protects the environment and ecology of the area and at the same time provides for the continuation of a time-honored Adirondack tradition.

The most spectacular areas of the Middle Branch are near the edge of the Blueline and somewhat difficult to access. These include a stunning waterfall, Rainbow Falls, and the "Tunnel," a striking gorge of pinkish granite gneiss through which the river flows beneath almost perpendicular walls. They are both in the Forest Preserve on easement lands and access is accordingly legal but still fairly difficult, requiring bushwhacking. This inaccessibility is amply compensated for by the wonders encountered upon arrival!

WEST BRANCH OSWEGATCHIE

Wild azalea, and its gorgeous blossoms that bestow both radiance and fragrance on a balmy May day, are what describes the West Branch most aptly. Their presence is quite rare in the Adirondack Park and in our area is limited to the banks of this river. I often ponder on the reasons for the rarity. A friend of mine successfully transplanted a young shrub from the river's bank to the hamlet of Fine. After two decades its blossoms continue to sparkle in spring.

A difference of opinion exists locally as to the true source of the West Branch. Both Hog Pond and Buck Pond have proponents, with the latter holding pride of place traditionally. Hog Pond, ringed with an esker and famous for the existence of a herd of feral pigs in the vicinity early in the twentieth century, also has its advocates, who have increased in number recently. The hogs, escapees from a lumber camp, survived for a number of years until the twin demons of harsh winters and rifle fire caught up with them.

Buck Pond, in my mind, will always be associated with the pine marten that we regularly fed in winter at a hunting camp located there until the 1980s. The camp's owner was Mike Virkler, who leased the land from International Paper Company for over half a century. I spent several nights at the camp with Mike and was treated to the pleasure of the marten's presence. Jelly, meat scraps, suet—they relished it all! Only one came when I was there, but Mike has seen three at a time (a family perhaps, female and two well-grown kittens). After the paper company sold the land to the state for inclusion in the Forest Preserve, Mike was allowed to stay on at the camp for an additional five years, at which time the camp was burned as per DEC policy. Sadly, an era came to an end. The supreme irony is that quite probably this was the only means available to ultimately protect the land for posterity.

One of the most striking gems of the West Branch is a trio of entrancing ponds just below Bergens, a small clearing in the forest that was the site of a rustic hotel catering mainly to hunters and operated by an elderly German couple. The ponds and surrounding lands are owned by the Future Farmers of America and are open, with some restrictions, to the public for boating and fishing. Brook trout are the order of the day here.

After leaving the Adirondack Park, the West Branch flows for approximately twelve miles through the Jadwin State Forest with only an occasional private holding intruding. Glimpses of wildlife are legion in this section, ranging across the spectrum from deer and beaver to wood ducks, with great blue herons forever, it seems, standing in the shallows seeking fish and frogs. Long stretches of the river below Jerden Falls are canoeable with only the odd beaver dam or fallen tree to overcome. The best put-in is from the bridge at Jerden Falls, which was once the site of a sawmill. The final take-out is at Kimballs Mill, a modest-sized cataract which in the previous era was also the setting for a sawmill and now-defunct hamlet that grew up around it. Some local people still persist in referring to the site by its prior name—Pigtown. This, of course, is frowned on officially.

The West Branch annexes the waters of the Middle Branch at the edge of the Jadwin State Forest and then proceeds through a more settled region until finally merging with the waters of the East Branch in the vicinity of Gouverneur. By then it has left the Great South Woods.

The Oswegatchie's branches and tributaries drain a substantial portion of the wild, wooded landscape of the northwestern Adirondacks. In fact, this watershed and the wilderness area it encompasses are the backbone of the proposed Bob Marshall Wilderness which has generated much discussion. The term "Greater Oswegatchie Forest" has been put forth as an alternate name for the concept in recognition of the fact that the area in question conforms approximately to the boundaries of the watershed for a considerable part of its territory.

RAQUETTE RIVER

"The river of the forest" it was called in a book written in the mid-1900s. It is most definitely still that today, while at the same time being a river of hydro dams, whitewater, and waterfalls. Wider than all other Adirondack rivers, it is the second longest river in New York State after the Hudson.

My memories of this river are as legion as the landscapes and waterscapes along its route. They are as diverse as the bald eagle soaring ubiquitously on a gentle summer breeze above the river, or feeding, along with others, on deer carcasses on the ice while fierce wintry blasts buffet all in sight. Otter are frequently sighted along this fish-laden river. I have one in mind who unabashedly peered at a group I was leading for a full ten minutes before disappearing through the ice with a seeming gesture of contempt. We were not much more than a pitcher's mound distance from him the whole time! Before his exit, we were entertained regally by his antics on the ice.

For me the Raquette River appears to be the river par excellence for the sighting of white-tailed does and their twin fawns. I often spy them on the banks of the river grazing and browsing contentedly, seemingly unperturbed by a passing canoeist.

Emerging from the sylvan sanctity of the High Peaks Wilderness Area and the Saranac Lake Wild Forest, the Raquette River enters St. Lawrence County at Piercefield Flow. Before this, its wilderness path has been interrupted, albeit only temporarily, by the outskirts of the hamlet of Tupper Lake, the largest village in the Adirondack Park.

Up river from Tupper Lake lie many delights I have become familiar with over the years. Raquette Falls, a wilderness cascade similar in

many respects to High Falls and, like it, a woodland hub, springs readily to mind. I often think of the secluded boarding house nationally famous for its pancakes that once stood by its shore. In less sublime mo-
ments of reminiscing, the patch of rare (for the Adirondacks) poison
ivy I encountered along the old truck trail into the falls comes to mind.

Unusual, too, for the Adirondacks is the wide, meandering floodplain lined with silver maples that marks the river's passage for miles
below the falls. In a day's paddle here, I nearly always enjoy the sight
or sound of wood ducks and blue-winged teal, in their own way enjoy-
ing the river every bit as much as I!

Part way through the reaches of the floodplain the outlet of Follensby Pond joins its waters to those of the Raquette River. Follensby
Pond, recent hack site of bald eagles and ancient site of the Philoso-
phers' Camp where Ralph Waldo Emerson and other luminaries held
forth in the stillness of nineteenth-century Adirondack evenings, was
once in the process of becoming part of the Forest Preserve, when the
owner suddenly changed his mind. If it ever does become part of the
preserve, it will make a splendid addition from both an ecological and
historical perspective.

Below Piercefield Flow and the adjoining hamlet of Piercefield, the
Raquette flows almost entirely through the Forest Preserve until just
before it enters Carry Falls Reservoir. This fifteen-mile stretch of river
is basically a whitewater canoe route, one of the most exhilarating in
the entire state. Scenic and scintillating as it may be, it is not without
its hazards and should only be undertaken with proper respect and
preparation. Two extended flatwater stretches along its route add variety to the trip. Interesting, too, is the remnant of an old logging bridge.
The bridge lent experience and challenge to a demolition crew from the
Fort Drum army base, who blasted it into oblivion a few years back.

Sol's Island, several miles below the dam at Piercefield, lies at the
confluence of the Raquette River and Dead Creek. Several hundred
acres in extent, Sol's Island is the largest of the many islands that dot
the river in this section. The island is named after a son of the legendary Peter Sabbatis, a member of the Abenaki nation, who figured
prominently in the early settlement of the Long Lake area. The wide
marshes of Dead Creek often reveal sightings of wildlife—great blue
herons and common snipe come immediately to mind. The island itself,

in addition to offering a number of attractive campsites, appears to be a natural attractant to the Eastern coyote. Their tracks in the sand along portions of the shore seem, at times, to rival in abundance those of cattle in the mud of a barnyard!

Moody Falls is the first of the two sizable cataracts along this stretch of river. It is mostly framed by the tall conifers of the Forest Preserve. As I have previously mentioned, legend states that a local log driver and his son attempted to run the falls and thereby achieved two things: 1) their instant demise, 2) immortality of a sort, the waterfall being named in their memory. Two things I usually notice here: 1) the abundance of avian life fly-catching, 2) the generally poor results fishing (on the few occasions I have been foolish enough to try). Still, the scenery is spectacular, the setting remote, and it's a good place to tarry before making the portage around the falls.

Jamestown Falls is the second waterfall along the river. Wider than high, Jamestown is bordered by the private lands of the Jamestown Club and also by the Forest Preserve. There are tall white pines here and an occasional hemlock, but mostly when I consider things arboreal I think of the red pine up slope a short distance from the bank. After much reflection, I'm still perplexed as to their origin—natural or planted? Makes for deep thinking on days when sightings of wildlife are scarce!

Below Jamestown Falls the river begins its protracted entrance into Carry Falls Reservoir. At well over 3,000 acres, Carry Falls is by far the largest of the many reservoirs on the Raquette. Also, as the first of five, it is the supplier of water for all the rest. At low water, sandy beaches are revealed all along the reservoir. While the annual drawdown inhibits and proves detrimental to some wildlife, others thrive in a setting both attractive and remote as well as giving the sense of being completely natural.

Just before the Raquette's entrance into Carry Falls some remnants of old-growth forest can be seen in the Forest Preserve parcels on the eastern shore. Some of the white pine and hemlock here are truly awesome, as is also the cryptic, hazy footpath that weaves its way furtively for miles through the forest.

The sight of bald eagles soaring here is one that never fails to send my spirit soaring along with them. I often sight them over the reservoir.

There is also an active nest on one of the downriver reservoirs and possibly another as-yet-undiscovered one in the vicinity.

Bats always seem to be skimming over the water surface here as dusk begins to unfold. On one memorable occasion they continued, flying all around as I frantically paddled toward shore during an electrical storm.

Northern pike and smallmouth bass thrive under the surface. There is even an occasional walleye, as one gentleman from North Creek can attest. I have crossed paths with him here at least half a dozen times, always casting for walleye from beneath the falls, always apparently successful!

At one time a rustic hamlet with the intriguing name of Hollywood was located in the vicinity. It ceased to exist when the rising waters of the reservoir enveloped it in the 1950s. It was named after a village in County Down, Ireland, rather than after the West Coast icon of the same name. Although it was submerged before my arrival in the Adirondacks, some of the surviving anecdotes suggest it had some of the whimsy of both its namesakes! All that remains today to attest to the fact that such a place existed are vestiges of the Old Hollywood Road, now primarily a woodland path, and some scattered cellar holes that belonged to structures on the village's outskirts. Try as I may, I have not yet found any sign of the ubiquitous day lily and lilac that were invariably planted around such buildings. I hope I do some day, for a living presence would be a much stronger memorial to the old hamlet!

SOUTH BRANCH GRASS RIVER

The South Branch of the Grass River is justly renowned as the river that hosts the most spectacular waterfalls in the entire Adirondack Park. It is almost equally renowned as a river of some confusion. The confusion has a dual nature, referring both to the correct spelling of the river's name and to the identity of the pond that is its source.

The river has been spelled at various times both with and without an "e" at the end. Those who claim the river was named for one of the early French explorers of the region opt for the "e"; others, claiming the river was named for the abundant aquatic eel grass so prevalent in stillwater stretches, prefer the name be spelled without it. In deference to local tradition and the example of the ultimate Adirondack paddler, Paul Jamieson, I have elected the spelling that refers to the local flora.

To add a little more complexity to the issue, both Center Pond and Sardine Pond have been described as the headwater of the Grass River. Tradition has accorded primacy of place to Center Pond, but a close perusal of the topo map will show that Sardine Pond is higher and thus could make the ultimate claim. For now, though, we'll leave the matter of the river's true origin to the theorists and keepers of records!

Recollections of the abundant flora and fauna on the wild stretches of this river are as varied as the leaf colors shining on an Adirondack hardwood hillside in the last week of September. The conifer-clad upper reaches of the river have provided sights ranging from magnificent swift-flying goshawks plucking unwary worm-searching robins off the forest floor to a supremely indifferent mink ambling along the shores of the river while a haranguing group of blue jays hovered over its head hurling every invective they could find in its direction. While saunter-ing on the shores, I often find that Canada jays will arrive precisely at lunch hour, often to take bread from my hand.

Memories of the lower river range from those enchanting, secluded sites where the wild butternut grows and the white trillium blooms, in all its glory, to the sight of the shimmering leaves of silver maple shak-ing in the wind just before a summer deluge. Memories of fauna are more muted here but nonetheless pleasant, be they of paddling along-side swimming beaver or securing a brown trout for a delicious supper under the pines.

The Grass begins life as a modest-sized stream for the first six miles as it flows through the lands of the Conifer Easement Tract. Marsh harriers soar over the corridor while a paddler has his progress impeded by many small beaver dams. I find the number of dams sur-prising as the river corridor here is fairly wide. However, it seems there are just enough alder here to provide material for construction of the dams. Some of the alders have a striking pattern of black and white scattered on their bark. The white, cottony masses are the over-wintering eggs of the aphid, while the black masses are a species of jelly fungus.

After its confluence with Burntbridge Pond Outlet, the Grass begins to assume the proportions of a small river and shortly thereafter flows through a sprawling peatland, Massawepie Mire. The peatland, technically classified as a fen, is owned mainly by a private club and is not open for public use. The black spruce and tamarack occurring here support one of the largest populations of the endangered spruce grouse in the entire Adirondacks. I have, on several occasions, heard spruce grouse calling while I was paddling on the river, but have never sighted the bird here. The only bird I ever sighted "wild" was the one I flushed from the base of a balsam fir in nearby Sevey's Bog, now also off-limits. Of course, I have had frequent close eyeball contact with the stuffed specimen previously on display for years at Dumas Restaurant in nearby Childwold.

The white tufts of cotton sedge waving in the breezes over the bog can be seen from the canoe. Also obvious are the shimmering red veins of the quaint leaf of the pitcher plant. All things wondrous and strange emanate from a bog.

After collecting the waters of Massawepie Lake Outlet, approximately halfway through the mire, the river becomes a little larger still. After the peatland comes the Grass River Flow, a large shallow pond formed by a small dam, beloved by bald eagles and Canada geese. The former I frequently see in summer, making me wonder if there is a nest in the vicinity. The latter have been nesting on the flow for decades and appear to be truly wild, in contrast to the geese on Tupper Lake and some other large lakes, which nevertheless have much of the feral about them.

The two miles of river extending from below the dam to Route 3 are mainly a series of rapids and flatwater stretches often impeded by log jams and beaver dams. There is a canoe takeout via Balsam Pond out to Route 3 a relatively short distance below the dam. The conifers lining this stretch furnish one of the largest deer yards in the entire Adirondack Park. In winter, coyotes, bald eagles, and ravens can frequently be seen here, ever intent on the deer yard. Snowshoe hares, too, appear incredibly abundant on this stretch. For me the river in this area is truly marked with magic!

The Grass then crosses under Route 3 and begins an approximate twenty-five-mile section to the rustic hamlet of Degrasse. This wondrous stretch is without doubt the crowning glory of the river in both wildness and scenic wonders. The brooding spruce and fir forests that line its entire route preside over a series of wild, rapturous waterfalls and rapids unrivaled in the entire Adirondack Park. Twin Falls, Rainbow Falls, Copper Rock Falls, Sinclair Falls—the names are legion and entrancing—each with its own essence and distinctive view. With the 1998 announcement by the governor concerning the purchase in fee and easement of the Champion Paper Company lands, the public at large can partake of the joys of this river gem which has, until now, been restricted to the sportsmen's club leasing the land from the paper company.

There is one stillwater stretch here, a pleasant eight-mile meander just below the Forest Preserve. The river crosses the Tooley Pond Road at the site of the abandoned hamlet of Newbridge. With the initial depletion of the area's natural resources, the reason for the hamlet's existence ceased and the remote location today is nothing more than a haunting reminder of things that were. The Tooley Pond Road itself, as bumpy and winding as a river as it proceeds along its lonely path, also evokes memories of a past now found only in ancient artwork.

Below the hamlet of Degrasse the river flows through a mixture of public and private lands to the semi-abandoned agricultural area around Russell. The public lands are themselves a mix of Forest Preserve and of managed State Forests as the river exits and then returns to the Adirondack Park. There is a charming four-mile canoe route from the Degrasse State Forest to the head of Lampson Falls in the Forest Preserve. Lampson Falls is currently the only one of the magnificent waterfalls adorning the South Branch of the Grass that is state-owned and protected. Sixty feet high and almost as wide, in the green season it is populated by cedar waxwings that flit and soar over the cascade of water as they endlessly scoop and swallow the hordes of mayfly hatch as they arise from the river. Both the Middle and North Branches of the Grass River are incorporated into the main river during this stretch; the former adds its waters in time to feed the nine tumbling cascades a mile below Lampson Falls.

The forest lining the banks of the river also undergoes a dramatic change below Degrasse. Basswood, lover of rich soil, and an occasional American elm begin to appear, as do silver maple and butternut. White pine and hemlock are still in evidence, but the more boreal spruce and fir have for the most part been left behind. The flora of the forest floor changes also; white trillium, hepatica, Dutchman's breeches and some of the entrancing spring ephemerals find the rich alluvial soil more to their liking and begin to flourish.

There is a dilemma here for me. Do I cherish more the brooding boreal fastness so prevalent along the upper river, or is the lively, more diverse and showy forest that denotes the lower river more to my liking? I have yet to resolve the matter. Miraculously, it appears to change depending on which section I visited last!

BOG RIVER

The Bog is a river of mystery and allure that lies in back of beyond. A river with two historic dams exuding glimpses of a lifestyle now utterly vanished. A river where the native moose lingered longest in the Adirondacks and where many a misguided "sportsman" of note made a frenzied effort to be the one to wipe this regal cervid from the map of New York State. All this and more can be said and felt of the Bog.

The river has furnished me with a host of memories and feelings over the years. The feeling of shame over the sordid episode of the moose, only now being erased with the gradual return of the forest monarch. Memories of osprey diving into Hitchins Pond and alighting with prized brook trout in their talons, of golden eagle soaring all summer long over the cliffs of the upper river and of startled otter plunging rapidly from the tops of glacial boulders where they were sunning themselves or feasting on freshwater mussels. The swiftness of their descent from the boulders to the underwater safety of the river at the approach of a canoe has to be seen to be believed.

Perhaps, however, the most vivid memory associated with Bog River fauna concerns not one of these more dramatic wildlife forms, but a much more humble one, the monarch butterfly. Sprinting swiftly to escape a sudden mid-September deluge, I took shelter under the overhanging eaves of the porch on the former Boy Scout residence at Hitchins Pond. From the safety of the porch I peered through the downfall and met with a startling sight. Clinging precariously to the huge blossoms of hydrangea bushes clumped before the house were monarch butterflies massed in the thousands! A conservative estimate would be a minimum of 20,000—a once-in-a-lifetime sight that I still treasure.

The two dams across the Bog were erected in 1903 and 1907 by Augustus A. Low of Brooklyn, New York, in furthering his diverse economic plans for the area. Low, at one time the proprietor of all in view, had a wondrous vision for his vast domain in the wilderness. For a time it even appeared his dream of development might come to fruition.

The prototype of an energetic turn-of-the-century entrepreneur, Low had the following enterprises operating here: bottled spring water being exported to urban areas; a sugarbush for maple syrup, the envy of all others in the East; and the harvesting and sale of the local wild berry crop for sale downstate. All this, of course, in addition to his extensive timbering operations, which formed the backbone for all his enterprises. Alas, it all came to naught as his domain slowly reverted to wilderness. Perhaps his chief memorial today is the commemorative plaque honoring him on top of the steep, brooding ledge overlooking Hitchins Pond and his former domain.

The dams have the effect of neatly dividing the river into three sections—an upper, middle, and lower. The lower section tumbles into Big Tupper Lake just below Bog River Falls, a charming cascade popular with local picnickers. Above the falls is a two-mile stretch of flatwater which can be paddled at leisure. Piles of mussel shells discarded by feeding muskrats are common along this stretch of river. The species of mussel often appears to be the attractive green paper mussel, in contrast to other areas of the Adirondacks where common brown mussel shells seem to be more in evidence.

Above this flatwater stretch lie slightly more than five miles of rippling rapids interspersed with shorter placid stretches to the lower dam. Interesting and entrancing as it may be to walk along the deer paths that meander under the canopy of the conifer-clad shores, the stretch is not favorable for paddling.

Above the lower dam, however, the river begins a smooth flow through a trough of granite ledges capped by an impressive stand of white pine. While not in the same league, perhaps, as some of the white pine ringing the banks of the Upper Oswegatchie, they are still impressive in their own right with the path of the river just made for the dip of a paddle.

After a while the river snakes its way through a sprawling, expansive marsh before arriving at the Upper Dam in three miles. Midway through the marsh, the Bog flows under a trestle of the fabled Adirondack Railroad.

The marsh never fails to elicit wildlife surprises: from the regular "stake-pumping" of the American bittern constantly reverberating throughout the marsh as the male calls his mate, to the ghostly apparition glimpsed through fog-shrouded mists of a large Eastern coyote swimming with all due vigor across Hitchins Pond, which lies adjacent to the marsh.

The Upper Dam was where an old lumberjack boarding house was located in the early 1900s. Later it became headquarters for the Boy Scout Council, which purchased this part of Low's domain before the state assumed ownership. In 1994 the edifice still stood, slowly crumbling and withering away all its grandeur to the elements. Replete with broken glass and scores of dead bats, it evokes in some a feeling of nostalgia for what was, but for others it is seen mainly as a hazard for the unwary.

Above the Upper Dam the path of the river is narrow for the first two miles as it is framed by high cliff-like ridges looming above it. Ravens seem to be continually calling from and soaring over these cliffs, accompanying paddlers on their way. About a mile from the dam the river is completely blocked by one of the entrancing gems of mystery peculiar to the Great South Woods—a floating "bog." Canoes have to be carried here, with care being taken to step gingerly across the sphagnum moss and pitcher plants of the bog.

After two miles the river opens up into an entirely different world. What had been the Bog River suddenly magnifies markedly and assumes the form of wide, sprawling Lows Lake. Littered with scenic islands having equally picturesque names such as Gooseneck and Frying Pan, Lows Lake receives the full brunt of the west winds along its entire length. Paddlers should exercise caution here, especially before a storm and during afternoons. Paddling along the shore at this time frequently reveals deer browsing, apparently totally unconcerned with any Homo sapiens in a canoe.

Low's Lake reputedly harbors one of the largest populations of breeding loons in the entire Adirondacks, along with nearby Cranberry Lake and Stillwater Reservoir. On a calm summer day their calls seem to reverberate across the entire lake. I have also seen golden eagles soaring here throughout the summer, both adults and the immature among their number. Since this area was the site of some of the last confirmed nesting of their species in the Adirondacks, it is often tempting to conjure images of an unknown nest hiding among the many cliffs that surround the lake.

The large flow brought about by the dam that created Lows Lake absorbed the waters of several ponds. Tomar Pond and Mud Pond now exist mainly as mementos on ancient maps, but Grassy Pond retains to this day an identity of its own. Connected by a wide channel to the main body of Lows Lake, it is rimmed by mountains including its namesake, Grassy Pond Mountain. The legendary Bob Marshall, while a student at the state ranger summer school on Cranberry Lake in the 1920s, frequently made this mountain his destination on some of the marathon hikes in the area for which he is now famed.

Tradition, legend, scenery, fauna—if one river can lay claim to it all, it is the river of mystery and history, the Bog!

VIII

PEAKS AND PONDS

Photo courtesy of Betsy Tisdale

Ampersand Mountain

The Great South Woods is a land singularly blessed in the bounteous supply of water strewn across its landscape. This water, in the form
of sparkling ponds and lakes, appears to be everywhere, usually in association with the area's many modest-sized mountains. Together they
define the essence of the Great South Woods and account for much of
its splendor and glory.

Rare indeed is the land that possesses both peaks and ponds in abundance. The presence of one often appears to preclude the other. The Great South Woods and the Adirondacks in general are truly unique in possessing both of these natural wonders in plenty.

Each of the two are relics of the last Ice Age which departed this area much later than it left most of the eastern United States. The ponds owe their origin to the glacial topography that resulted directly from the recession of the ice, while the peaks were sculpted by and received their present shape from the very movement of that ice.

The landscape as it appears today, when viewed from on high, seems to be comprised of myriad ponds and lakes sprawling over the surface. Looming everywhere over the ponds are a series of low, rounded mountains that seem to envelope the landscape in all directions. In some cases the ponds and peaks are so inexorably linked together that their very names reflect this linkage. Often in these cases the ponds lie at the bases of the peaks.

All, ponds and peaks, have a feel of their very own with their own distinctive character shining through. In addition, the fauna and flora of each are often quite distinct and leave their own mark on the landscape.

I first became familiar with these peaks and ponds during the course of numerous hunting and fishing forays. Later, in the course of writing ADK's *Trail Guide to the Northern Adirondacks,* I attained an even more intimate awareness of their glory. Most of them have marked trails leading to them (as outlined in the guide). The order listed here is rather random, but they are roughly grouped according to size. All have provided me with untold enjoyment and a sense of wonder over the years. I hope I can now transfer some of that enjoyment and wonder to the reader.

PEAKS

The peaks span, in elevation, from barely 2,000 feet to over 3,400 feet. Their tops are mostly bare for a variety of reasons, all of them human in origin, such as clearing for the erection of fire towers early in the twentieth century as well as for the land surveying activities of the fabled Verplanck Colvin in the nineteenth century. As with the ponds, I have tried to give as representative a sample as possible of the peaks that occur here.

AMPERSAND MOUNTAIN

Ampersand Mountain, for me, will always be associated with the metal plaque embedded into the bedrock on its top commemorating Walter Rice, who was for years the official fire tower observer on Ampersand. This same Walter Rice was the mentor of author Martha Reben and is mentioned throughout her two charming books on this area of the Adirondacks.

Perhaps the most outstanding fact about Ampersand Mountain is the truly old-growth forest that mantles its base and its mid-elevation areas. These stands consist of a beech/maple and a hemlock/northern hardwood component and form a splendid setting for the first section of the trail. Indian cucumber root and sarsaparilla are resplendent in bloom under the full-leaf canopy of summer, while the gorgeously eerie purple buds of red elder so noticeable in late winter never fail to conjure up latent memories of Druids and such in my active subconscious.

In caves just beneath the summit, almost invariably patches of snow linger in areas of shade, sometimes well into June. The summit itself is approximately 3,400 feet in elevation, but appears much higher due to the steepness and roughness of the terrain.

On the top my thoughts also turn to the wild, trailless Seward Range, clearly visible several miles to the south. Almost always those thoughts seem to center on what hidden creatures may yet roam this secluded range unimagined by adherents of orthodox science.

DeBAR MOUNTAIN

DeBar Mountain is noticeable from quite a distance, looming starkly and impressively over the forests of Franklin County. So memorable is this distant view and so dominating that it has given its name to the entire extensive breadth of the state wild forest surrounding it.

Once on top, I have to admit that I find the view a classic case of the promise hinting more than the fulfillment. This is particularly true when compared with other Adirondack peaks, which while not so dominating from a distance, still manage to give a more expansive view on top. DeBar's isolation in a relatively level area of terrain probably accounts for this prominence from a distance and the correspondingly greater expectation of the view on top.

This 3,300-foot mountain disappoints in little else, however. The sense of wildness enveloping as you ascend is all-pervasive. Signs of wildlife abound and the cliff areas along the climb are reputed locally to be the focus of an abundant bobcat (and perhaps other feline) population. They certainly look it.

The foundations of the old fire tower are still present on top and hark back to memories of an era long vanished. DeBar's somewhat small twin, Baldface Mountain, is very much in evidence across a wooded valley. Baldface is trailless, but can be bushwhacked from County Route 99. The underlying rock must have quite a bit of calcium in it for I frequently notice plants that generally require sweeter soil. Among those that are quite common are yellow jewelweed and Christmas fern.

And, on top, the solitude and sense of wildness, even minus the classic panoramic view, is unsurpassed as a tonic for the soul.

ST. REGIS MOUNTAIN

In St. Regis we come to a moderate-sized peak that seems to dominate the surrounding area from every direction. No matter from what angle viewed, this modest peak appears to tower above the low-lying ponds, peatlands, and conifer forests that roll away from its foot. The name links the mountain, along with several large lakes and a river, to give testimony to the Native American tribe that had hunting camps in the area for thousands of years.

A 3.4-mile, relatively heavily used trail leads to the summit where an unmanned fire tower still stands. Large glacial erratics and an impressive stand of ancient sugar maple define the forest on the way up. Chalky white birch and stunted spruce come into evidence just before the top. From the top the High Peaks and the wild and trailless Seward Range can be clearly seen to the south. Brooding DeBar Mountain is equally obvious guarding the northeastern reaches of the region.

The view is splendid, the forest magnificent; but mostly when my thoughts turn to St. Regis Mountain they turn to Camp Topridge, nestled below on the shores of the striking Spectacle Ponds. Topridge was for years the home of the cereal heiress Marjorie Merriweather Post and her Russian nobleman husband. It was one of the most splendid of the Adirondack Great Camps and one of the few open to the public, albeit temporarily, when it was owned by New York State as a retreat and conference center for the governor. I first became aware of Camp Topridge when members of the Five Ponds Wilderness Citizens' Advisory Committee were given a guided tour of the estate prior to its being open to the public.

Subsequently, the state sold Camp Topridge, starting a donnybrook as many local environmentalists stated that the sale was in violation of the New York State Constitution. The new owner, an enigmatic Atlantic City entrepreneur named Roger Jakubowski, proceeded to stir things up further by postulating publicly and often on what a great place for development the Adirondacks was. Mr. Jakubowski left, however, after a short tenure and relatively benign treatment of the land.

The camp, under new ownership, still slumbers at the foot of the mountain. It zealously guards its many secrets and the strife that is but a memory today.

CAT MOUNTAIN

Nestled in the wooded folds of the Five Ponds Wilderness, Cat Mountain has memories most varied for me. The base of the fire tower, erected in 1911, is still very visible on the summit, as is the foundation of the fire observer's cabin just below. The fire observer was John Janack and at the landing on Dead Creek Flow below the mountain he raised eleven children. The feel of that era now gone is oft felt here still, especially on a windless summer day. It is enhanced by the solitary apple tree yet remaining on top and by day lilies, once so carefully planted, which to this day send forth their blossoms all through the summer. These vestiges are all that remain of the first fire tower built in the Adirondack Park.

During the 1970s there was a period when the only known raven nest in New York State was on the steep cliffs of Cat Mountain. I have vivid recollections of these ravens sallying forth from the cliff to harass and strike a turkey vulture who was sailing by. I watched in wonder as they repeatedly struck at the turkey vulture, ultimately driving it away.

The ravens no doubt recognized a threat to their young as well as the possibility of their nesting site itself being usurped by the turkey vulture. I have to add that the final exit of the vulture from the scene was entirely devoid of any nobility!

As a destination Cat Mountain was more popular in the earlier part of the century. Guides would take their urban clients who were staying at the hotels and lodging houses up the mountain for a brisk and refreshing day trip. It was during this time that the mountain reportedly received its name, after the sighting of a cougar by a group making the climb. I have been told by two friends that they have glimpsed an elusive cat on two separate occasions ascending the peak during the past decade. I believe both of them.

The view on top reveals, as nothing else can, the vastness and wildness of the Five Ponds Wilderness Area as wooded ridge after wooded ridge stretches to the horizon with nary a sight of any man-made intrusion to interrupt the magic.

BEAR MOUNTAIN

This mountain is quite singular in one aspect: it is the only one of those mentioned here that is entirely wooded on its summit. A rock outcrop beyond the summit does give a view, however.

Bear Mountain is also notable for the quality of the forest that climbs up its slopes. This is in essence an old-growth hardwood stand with magnificent specimens of sugar maple and yellow birch. These two species, in which the bark is so different in their early years, are difficult to distinguish as they approach old age because the bark of the yellow birch assumes a shaggy appearance like the maple's. I have to look closely to separate the two in the ancient specimens of up to three hundred years old that are common here. One sure way is the presence of huge, round cankers on many of the old yellow birch. Scientists debate whether a fungus or a bacteria is the causative agent, but I am content to appreciate the size of these cankers and their seeming harmony with the parent birch.

Beech scale disease has killed most of the larger beech here, opening considerable gaps in the canopy. A thick growth of saplings has responded to the increase in sunlight. The demise of one specific beech is vividly etched in my memory. It picked the time it takes to trek two hundred feet to topple over the stretch of trail I had just trod! A dual recognition then ensued of the power and awesome grandeur of a falling forest monarch and of the incredible luck of an unwary hiker!

A cozy rustic lean-to erected by the county's Youth Conservation Corps is located half way up the trail. This is a pleasant place to enjoy a rest under a handsome stand of pole-sized white pines.

The view on the 2,180-foot summit embraces most of Cranberry Lake with its numerous islands as well as duplicates the view from Cat Mountain of wild, wooded ridges stretching seemingly ad infinitum. One of those ridges, located two miles south and several hundred feet higher, is also named Bear Mountain. This trailless Bear Mountain attests both to a limited imagination on the part of early peak-namers and also to the super abundance of berry-consuming bruins locally.

For me, however, perhaps the highlight of this mountain is the sight of the autumn hawk migration that may be had from the ledge outcrop on a fine September day. A bevy of raptors, mainly broad-winged hawks, soar on the thermal currents on these very special days and proclaim by their grace and beauty that all is right with the world!

MOUNT ARAB

Mount Arab looms large over the wild woodlands of the eastern edge of the Great South Woods. From the top one can see the water tower looming over the village of Tupper Lake as well as endless forested ridges and ponds rolling to the horizon. Fantastic views, an exotic name, and charming ponds at its foot including a namesake lake: Mount Arab is all this and more, but when I think of Mount Arab my thoughts turn to "Woody," the fire tower observer who spent several decades manning this outpost until his retirement in the 1980s.

I learned a lot from discussions with Woody on top of the 2,500-foot mountain. Often we had to hastily abandon the fire tower, built in 1918, as flaming bolts of lightning began to strike all around us. Woody stated that in all his time on top of the mountain, he had never seen a coyote or signs of them up that high. Red foxes galore, both sight and sign, but never a glimpse of a coyote. I thought this strange at the time but since then, in scores of trips up the mountain, I have seen numerous scat and an occasional track, all attributable as far as I could determine to fox. The learning process never ceases!

Stunted red spruce and mountain ash grow on top, fringing the bare rock at the very crown. The fire tower still stands, albeit in an increasingly decrepit state. The stairs have been removed, but intrepid, foolish types still manage to ascend it. The observer's cabin, too, still stands. It's even more decrepit than the tower itself for the onslaught of vandals has been more furious against the cabin. Interesting, too, is the quantity of porcupine spoor that litters the inside. This bears witness to the well-known penchant of porcupines to search out abandoned buildings for shelter.

I continue to trek to the top of Mount Arab at least a dozen times a year. My dream is to one day surprise his royal majesty, the red fox, up there for myself.

AZURE MOUNTAIN

Nestled in isolation from all other Adirondack peaks, Azure Mountain is much beloved by the hiking community in the Potsdam-Canton area. It was one of the original hacking sites for the re-introduction of the peregrine falcon in New York. The memories of the hacking platform and young graduate students who fed the falcons here and strove to protect them from any harm are still fresh in my memory.

A memory even more vibrantly alive is the time I surprised a black bear feeding, in late August, in the pin cherry and chokecherry thickets that are so abundant on the mountain's crest. The bear fortunately went over the other side of the crest in just about the same flash it took my gut feelings to progress from awe to palpitation. I was not really that surprised at this encounter, for I had often observed bear sign on the summit. The bears are attracted no doubt by the cherries as well as shadberry, which also thrives on top.

The summit has its share of stunted spruce as befits all the low mountains of the Great South Woods. The bare bedrock here harks back to the surveying triangulations of the 1800s under the guidance of Verplanck Colvin. Moving around on the face of the peak gives a view of the St. Regis River as well as the extensive woodlands that surround it in all directions.

I search in vain for the falcon, but often am rewarded by the sight of ravens and turkey vultures performing their version of aerial acrobatics. A sight certainly worth the modest trek to the top!

DOG POND MOUNTAIN

Dog Pond Mountain is a tiny peak almost completely surrounded by a throng of other peaks, most of which are higher than it—sort of landlocked, if such can apply to a peak.

While this is not an overly impressive resumé, the mountain itself is a pleasant surprise. A short trek through a handsome forest from the Dog Pond Loop leads to a charming overlook on the side of the mountain. The view is not panoramic but gives a detailed glimpse of Center Pond and its environs, so intimate that it almost feels like a personal close-up.

Bear Mountain rears up above Dog Pond Mountain, adding to its mystique. This is not the Bear Mountain adjacent to the lake, but another one approximately three forested miles away. A paucity of eligible names in the last century perhaps?

The mountain itself was named after a canid that was killed on the shores of Dog Pond late last century. In retrospect it appears the creature was actually a hybrid—part wolf and part domestic dog. With so many "Wolf Mountains" and "Wolf Lakes" around, those who christened the pond and mountain probably felt they were bestowing individuality with their naming.

An overlook is reached just below the forested 2,440-foot summit. The intimate view, a splendid stand of white birch and a stunning rock overhang combine to define the mountain.

FREDERICA MOUNTAIN

This is another remote little peak with a splendid, albeit decidedly localized, view. Local it may be, but it is completely unsurpassed in the intimate, personal glimpse it provides of Lake Lila sprawling below.

For years a private lean-to was located upon the 2,240-foot summit, clearly showing that others appreciated the views also. The others, of course, were the Webb family, landowners and railroad builders. The

Frederica for whom the peak is named was a member of that family.

It was while making the short trek up to the summit that I happened to hear the only vocalization from a black bear that I've ever heard in all the myriad miles I've trod in the forests of the Great South Woods. I inadvertently got in between a sow and her cubs and the female uttered a hoarse grunt several times in a row. Whether a bluff or not, the element of warning was readily apparent and I believe I made the ascent in record time.

Although the above encounter eclipses all others when I think of Frederica Mountain, I'm not tempted to change the name. Frederica can rest assured she will still be honored. After all, how many pinnacles can we have in one woods commemorating a single member of the fauna?

PANTHER MOUNTAIN

A tiny mountain easily accessible from the Tupper Lake-Saranac Lake highway, Panther Mountain is surprisingly often overlooked. The view on top, while not panoramic, does give a glimpse into the wild Seward Range several miles away and on an especially clear day the High Peaks can be seen off in the distance. Like many of its kindred peaks, Panther Mountain has a namesake pond nestled at its foot; a tiny, circular pond that has special regulations restricting the use of live bait when fishing for brook trout. The trout have little to fear from me, however; I have struck out on three occasions fishing here.

Truly noble specimens of spruce and hemlock line the short trail to the summit. The forest here certainly looks like it might be old-growth. In the summer, it seems I can always count on finding a striking emerald green locust hopping all over the top of the bare rock. Its presence is as guaranteed here as the U.S. Geological Survey markers and the showy mountain ash. I can't recall noticing this handsome insect elsewhere. Is this from a lack of focused observation on my part or is this locust truly an endemic species restricted to Adirondack mountain tops? The verdict is still out.

In contrast to Mount Arab, I have seen signs of Eastern coyote up high here. It was early December with several inches of snow blanketing the ground. Tracks of at least five of these large canids went over a high shoulder of the mountain apparently just for excitement because there was no sign of deer and little of hare. All of a sudden from down in the ravine beneath the aspens, the pack let forth a thrilling, weird medley of yips, barks, and howls. This was the classic pack howl, still two hours before dusk. The sound was especially loud, uncanny and prolonged even when measured with other coyote serenades I've been treated to.

From that time on, tiny, overlooked Panther Mountain became just a little more special in my estimation!

PONDS

The ponds in the Great South Woods range in size from several acres to several thousands of acres. Their depth and the species of fish present also very widely. Color ranges from the brown imparted by the tannin of decaying conifer needles to the deep blue that reflects the clarity of the sky. A few are emerald green, a result I believe of certain minerals present in them. All were created by natural processes, foremost of which was the activity of the relatively recently departed glacial ice.

STILLWATER RESERVOIR and CRANBERRY LAKE

These two large, sprawling bodies of water define the approximate geographic boundaries of the Great South Woods, at least on a north-south axis. Both of these substantial lakes had their original size considerably enhanced with the construction of dams around the turn of the century. The similarity extends to their shorelines, most of both now in the Forest Preserve.

They both are wonderful for canoe camping and I have spent countless pleasurable hours paddling them and observing wildlife on their waters, shores, and islands. There is a hazard here—both are subject to the full brunt of the prevailing westerly winds, particularly in the afternoon. On several occasions I had to paddle mightily to reach shore when winds increased their velocity dramatically and suddenly! In addition, motorboat use is heavy on both and swamping has to be avoided.

Another interesting linkage between the two lakes is the fact that high levels of mercury have been found in some of the fish inhabiting their waters. This, of course, is a direct result of the acid precipitation that has ravaged the area's waters and forests in recent decades. Hence we are presented with the anomaly of otherwise pristine bodies of water in a relatively primeval setting being afflicted with the negative residue of modern civilization.

Stillwater Reservoir, at 6,700 acres, one time had the distinction of having the lowest officially recorded temperature ever taken in New York State. This was a frigid -52° F in the 1930s, a record that was tied in nearby Old Forge in 1979.

I prefer summer with its breeding loons, the second largest colony in the Adirondacks, and the bald eagles and osprey constantly hovering overhead. Perhaps they have their eye on the splake swimming below the surface. A hybrid of brook trout and lake trout, they provide some good angling. Then, too, the breeding pair of cormorants come readily to mind. They were first pointed out to me by Terry Perkins, the ranger at Stillwater for several decades. It is unusual to find cormorant away from the Great Lakes.

Cranberry seems still to have the memory of famed novelist Irving Bacheller and artist Frederic Remington lingering on its wild shores. They both frequented these shores around the turn of the century. At approximately 7,000 acres, its breeding pairs of loons rival Stillwater's for bragging rights. Herring gulls nest on some rock islands in the lake, another linkage with the Great Lakes. Canada geese nest on some of the "flows," flooded inlets created by the dam erected late in the 1800s. Osprey and bald eagles also nest nearby, seeking the brook trout that survived the onslaught of the introduced yellow perch earlier in the century. With a little imagination I can even conjure up the cranberries that were present before the dam flooded them out!

LAKE LILA

As spectacular as this sprawling lake is, its grandeur is often eclipsed by the fact that it is as hard to reach as any Adirondack lake that can be driven to. Access is achieved by a very narrow, six-mile-long gravel right-of-way from the Sabbatis Road.

Upon arrival, the sense of the spectacular is overwhelming. At approximately 1,400 acres, Lake Lila is the largest lake wholly contained in the Forest Preserve.

Lake Lila's cup of natural wonders truly overflows at the rim. Seven pristine islands, each possessing its own uniqueness. One thing they all have in common, in addition to spruce and pine, is the calling loons out on the water that are guaranteed to serenade the awakening camper in the morning. Ospreys nest, lake trout and land-locked salmon lurk in the depths, and Lake Lila boasts its own sparkling natural sand beach.

It also had, standing on its shores for decades, one of the most famous of the Adirondack Great Camps. The camp had been built by the Webb family and was truly a wonder to behold. I feel fortunate in having seen it on two occasions before the DEC had to burn it in accordance with the state mandate that prescribes this fate for any edifice existing on a parcel upon its absorption into the Forest Preserve. The last time I saw the structure standing, I had the unsettling feeling that somehow it was aware of the fate that shortly awaited it!

A hermit trapper by the name of Smith was the first European of record to dwell along the shores of Lake Lila. The lake and the modest-sized mountain overlooking it were named originally after him. When the Webb family subsequently acquired the lake and adjoining woodlands as part of their 100,000-acre domain in the 1800s, the lake and mountain were renamed to honor two female members of the Webb family. They are—Lake Lila and Frederica Mountain. Even so, some still speak today of sensing the aura of a nineteenth-century hermit in their treks to this remote wilderness lake.

SALMON LAKE

It is usually toward the end of the day when I finally arrive at Salmon Lake. The afternoon may be waning and my bones even aching a bit, but the sight of Salmon Lake never fails to re-invigorate my spirit and rekindle electricity in my body.

The reasons for this are as varied as the species of trees in the old-growth forest that surrounds the lake. The most obvious is the enchantingly wild aspect the lake presents in its remoteness. This enchantment for a 110-acre body of water that lies sprawling amidst such surrounding grandeur is perhaps inevitable.

Other factors add to this feeling of intoxication. They range from the lunker native lake trout lurking in the depths of the lake to the path itself, the fabled Red Horse Trail that figured so prominently in the early woodland lore of the entire region.

Whatever the reasons, the sense of enchantment never fails to manifest itself. Solitude, remoteness, wildness, even a glimpse of the past all combine to cause subconscious feelings normally deeply submerged to surface rapidly and unexpectedly.

In addition to lake trout, there is another uncommon boreal species of fish present in the deep waters of Salmon Lake. The lake chub has co-evolved with the lake trout ever since the last glacier relaxed its frigid grip some 10,000 years ago. They are truly glacial relics every bit as much as the glacial boulders scattered through the surrounding forest.

I frequently spy loons on the surface of the lake. Invariably it is not long before they dive beneath the surface for nourishment. Often I wonder what the dining bill of fare could be here. While wondering I am also fervently hoping that the two glacial relics are decidedly sparse in the diet of the diving water birds.

SAND LAKE

Sand Lake is in many respects the ultimate in remoteness. At least it is as remote as a lake can be and still be reached by trail—thirteen wonderful miles through the Oswegatchie forest from the trailhead at Wanakena!

Upon arrival at this sparkling seventy-two-acre body of water, the intrepid traveler is greeted by the sight of mammoth white pines towering over the lake and the enticing natural sand beach along part of its shoreline. The famous Five Ponds Esker separates Sand Lake from mysterious Rock Lake, which beckons from its other side.

Despite being surrounded by all this natural splendor, my thoughts invariably turn to a human dimension when I think of Sand Lake. On one occasion I met a couple from Pennsylvania fly fishing on the Oswegatchie River above High Falls. They were catching trout in abundance but were quick to bemoan the modest size of their quarry. I, never being able to keep a secret, directed them to Sand Lake. Several months later I received a letter sent to me through the publishers of my trail guide, the Adirondack Mountain Club. The couple not only caught trout at Sand Lake, but included among the take were several four-pound lunkers. They were ecstatic and so, to tell the truth, was I.

Even more poignantly associated with Sand Lake for me is the memory of Ann and Bob Munro of Wanakena. This couple, in their own quiet and unassuming fashion, had climbed all the peaks not only in the Adirondacks but in the Catskills and New England as well. While doing this they had acquired a lore and knowledge of the wild woodlands that was second to none. They sent a pleasant letter to me tactfully pointing out the fact that the first edition of my trail guide had inadvertently neglected to mention the fact that a lean-to was located at Sand Lake. Thanks to this timely reminder I was able to rectify this omission in a subsequent issue of *Adirondac* magazine by pointing out to the readers that the lean-to was still present to greet the weary hiker at the conclusion of thirteen marvelous miles!

After this the Munros and I became warm friends. Bob, an avid fly fisherman also, was able to assist me with information when I wrote a chapter on fishing the Oswegatchie River for a book on Adirondack fishing. I have a strong feeling that they're watching fondly over the forest they so loved from their abode in the sky!

OTTER POND

This secluded forty-three-acre body of water nestled amidst one of the largest stands of old-growth hardwoods in the entire Adirondack Park has much to recommend. However, when my thoughts turn to Otter Pond they focus on the illicit hunting camp that blissfully stood for years on its shore, seemingly sacrosanct from the minions of the law.

It was a warm September day when I first became acquainted with the camp. A companion and I had paddled two miles up the Oswe-gatchie River to the point of its confluence with the alder-choked Otter Pond Outlet. We then succumbed to the brilliant notion of paddling up the outlet to its source in Otter Pond.

After carries over thirty-two beaver dams in one and one half miles, we finally reached our destination. Instead of the pristine and primitive ambiance we had expected, considering the difficulty of reaching the pond, we were, to the contrary, confronted by the sight of a rustic two-room hunting camp on the far shore as we pulled over the last mammoth beaver dam at the pond's outlet. As rustic and evocative as the camp was, it instantly dispelled any notion that we were the first ever to set eyes on this out-of-the-way lough!

The pair of loons strenuously calling on the pond allayed some of our disappointment. Finding two previously unknown ponds on an inlet of Otter Pond also helped in this regard. The two had beaver activity on them, but apparently they did not owe their origin to the work of the beaver but rather of the glacier.

The camp bestowed a touch of nostalgia on the pond. It was heavily used and not just by its original builders. Local woodsmen frequently utilized it to stop for a snack and to seek shelter in inclement weather. I confess to partaking of its comfort several times myself.

The existence of the camp was part of the local legend and lore at the DEC branch office in Canton. On several occasions small groups set out to locate it and determine who the owners were. Their efforts were for naught, for upon arriving at the pond they were unable to find any camp, for it was located behind a peninsula on the end of the lake. The natural lay of the land dictated that anyone seeking to reach the pond would, in the normal course of travel, arrive at the foot of the lake. From here the camp was completely invisible!

What of the fate of the camp? I've been informed by officials that it has been dismantled at last. Although I've been back to the pond several times since being told, I haven't had the heart to seek out the camp. Something far deep in my psyche whispers to me that I'll be disappointed no matter what the situation is!

CRYSTAL LAKE

This fourteen-acre body of emerald-colored water presents me with a dilemma. Locally it is famous for two different reasons. My thoughts on the lake turn equally to both!

One source of fame is the fact that it served as the private swimming hole for Andrew Shuler when he had his personal fiefdom in these environs. He had sand imported all the way from Niagara Falls and spread on the shores of the pond. The beach remains to this day, but the long wooden pier installed at that time has long succumbed to the ravages of time.

Still, area natives widely utilize the pond as their own swimming hole. I fondly recall the many hazy summer days enjoyed here with my own family. My children have graduated from college now, but never cease to inquire as to how things are at Crystal Lake.

The other reason Crystal Lake is renowned in local lore is the fact that it has never supported a viable population of fish going back to the earliest days of settlement. Certain minerals make the pond's natural level of acidity greater than what can be tolerated by members of the piscatorial clan. This is in contrast to the artificially high pH levels which acid precipitation has visited upon some local water bodies recently. The difference lies primarily in the origin—natural vs. anthropomorphic. The results are the same—fish cannot survive in these waters for any length of time.

The incredible clarity of the water in Crystal Lake bespeaks this high level of acidity. So too, in a way, does the wonderful buoyancy encountered when swimming. It's almost like being in salt water, which is not surprising considering the minerals which have produced the above effects in the first place.

Fish may not be present but this apparently does not deter loons, which I notice fairly often on this pond. Various crustaceans and aquatic insects appear to substitute for fish here. Apparently, enough of them are present to make it worthwhile for loons to explore this pond, which in the normal course of events would be too small for their presence. I once watched with rapt fascination as an energetic loon took off from the surface of the water. It had to traverse the entire width of the pond before it finally gained enough momentum for a takeoff.

To endure a close call like this, the dining must be truly elegant!

NICK'S POND

There are two Nick's Ponds in the Great South Woods. Both are linked by the Forest Preserve and by the name of the man they commemorate.

Nick Glasby was a nineteenth-century hunter and trapper who roamed these primeval woods unfettered and free. I've been unable to find out much else about Nick Glasby except that he much preferred the solitude of the big woods to the lure of the settlements that were beginning to appear locally.

One pond is hardwood-fringed and located a stone's throw from a gravel road in the Cranberry Lake Wild Forest. The other, deep in the bosom of the Five Ponds Wilderness, is not reached until after a hike of eight miles. The latter has traditionally been the destination of hunting parties using mules to backpack their equipment in. In addition to the hardwoods, large specimens of white pine and hemlock also guard its shore.

It is the Nick's Pond close to civilization that holds the bulk of wildlife memories for me. So many and so spectacular for a thirteen-acre pond adjacent to a road! This is the pond where a tail-slapping beaver and a shore-bound black bear put on their performance for me one unforgettable June afternoon. Eclipsing even this splendid sight, however, are the cumulative views that otter have shared with me on this pond down through the years. If such an entity as otter heaven exists, Nick's Pond is surely it!

On its water and along its shores I've watched otter sliding and tumbling, snarling and fighting, bobbing and weaving as they raised their heads above the surface of the water all the while inspecting me. Especially memorable is one otter who continually broke the thin April ice as it shot its head through it and uttered a series of indecipherable grunts. These were without a doubt directed at me but their purpose totally eluded me. Maybe the otter knew something I didn't!

BALSAM POND

This is a classic kettle pond surrounded by a typical bog mat and ringed with a pine-studded esker. The special charm of Balsam Pond lies in its intimate proportions and its proximity to a state highway. These attributes lend to it easy and intensive exploration, an acquaintanceship easily made and, once made, tending to last. The presence of the South Branch of the Grass River on the other side of the esker increases the appeal of this cozy little pond. The appeal does not wane even when the blueberry bushes that are so prominent on the northern shore invariably fail to produce any fruit. The heavy shade usually prevents flowering and, hence, fruiting. The glorious flaming crimson color of the bushes come September will have to suffice as far as the blueberries are concerned!

I remember vividly one late December day as I followed the tracks of a Canada lynx from one part of the pond to the other and over the esker into an adjoining spruce forest. The track was recently made and my heart clicked with palpitation as I wildly anticipated perhaps catching a glimpse of this magnificent feline. The advent of darkness precluded this, however.

I eagerly returned early the next morning to resume the pursuit. It was all in vain, however, as a fresh two inches of snow had fallen overnight in Cranberry Lake. I was chagrined since no snow had fallen overnight on my home turf of Fine.

My disappointment was considerably lessened, however, by the track that was present in the freshly fallen snow. Clearly etched before my eyes was the track of an adult bear proceeding in approximately the same direction as the lynx track the day before. The date was December 23, two days before Christmas, and the latest I had ever seen evidence of a bear being out and about in the winter. Why was this bear not in hibernation? I'm not sure. That year (1994) many bears went into hibernation quite late. I like to think that possibly it delayed hibernation that winter so I could note the track and write about it. More likely that warm weather and a paucity of food accounted for the delay!

IX

THE TREES

Photo courtesy of Duncan Cutter
White birch

An old adage proclaims that the forest often can't be seen for the trees. There is a ring of truth in this statement as far as the Great South Woods are concerned. The aura of the individual trees is occasionally so powerful that at times it can obscure the essence of the forest. With just a cursory glance even the magnificent old growth so prevalent here takes a back seat to the stature of pine, the white of birch, and the aroma of fir.

An exciting and diverse mix of individual tree species has established themselves locally since the relatively recent recession of the last glacier. They are the backbone of the Great South Woods and the most visible members of the flora. In addition, they are probably also the most important single element in the entire Adirondack ecosystem. Indeed, except for wetlands, water, recently disturbed areas, and the eighty acres of alpine tundra, the Adirondacks are covered almost completely with them.

The following brief sketches of individual tree species are portraits of their images as retained in my senses. The trees listed are the most prominent members of the forest and contribute in a measurable manner to the functioning of that forest. They dominate the landscape in varying degrees. All are native except for the exotic Scotch pine, which has managed to forge an identity for itself as a minor component of the Great South Woods. A few trees of marginal size and/or peripheral occurrence have been omitted.

RED SPRUCE

Red spruce is the conifer most intimately associated with the Adirondacks, from both an historical and an ecological perspective. It was one of the major components of the nineteenth-century forest; and its relentless pursuit by lumbermen of that era led to the opening of much of the region to settlement. Extremely shade-tolerant, red spruce makes excellent growth in the region and was formerly abundant along watercourses, in swamps, on lower slopes, and on the ridge crests of the area's low mountains. Unfortunately it does not regenerate as efficiently as some hardwoods and so today is much less common than in the past. With the "forever wild" provision of the Forest Preserve lands, that situation is happily changing, quite slowly but surely.

Old-growth red spruce can be seen along the Five Ponds trail to Sand Lake and on the esker above Cage Lake. Not as tall or massive as white pine or hemlock, they are still truly impressive in their own right. Scattered virgin red spruce can, in addition, be found throughout the Cranberry Lake Wild Forest west of the hamlet of Cranberry Lake.

Spruce die-back, reflecting a wide spectrum of causes including acid rain, is causing mortality of red spruce in the High Peaks area of the Adirondacks, but so far appears not to be a problem in the Great South Woods.

Formerly, the resin produced by red spruce, as an antidote for injury to the tree, was used as a source of gum and provided the basis for a minor local industry. Gum pickers harvested the resin from the spruce in winter and took it to the hamlet of Russell, where a gum factory was located earlier in the twentieth century. The resultant product was sold all over the East in the days before chicle became the main source of commercial gum. I have tasted the gum and found it does indeed produce a pleasant taste, but only after intensive chewing!

Red spruce has a low appeal as browse for white-tailed deer. I find it the least utilized by deer as food during winter, although there is a decided abundance of the tree in the typical Adirondack deer yard. Red squirrels, on the other hand, extensively utilize the seeds within the spruce cones as food and, in addition, have a noticeable tendency to build their globular leaf nests high up in the boughs. Black bears, too, are attracted to red spruce almost as much as balsam fir for leaving their territorial claw marks on its bark.

These hills wouldn't be Adirondack without red spruce!

YELLOW BIRCH

Yellow birch is, in many respects, the hardwood most intimately associated with the Adirondack forest. It not only attains some of its best growth in the Adirondacks, but also appears nearly ubiquitous, growing equally well with red spruce and hemlock in the cool "flats" and thriving on the slopes alongside beech and sugar maple.

As yellow birch ages it increasingly assumes a hoary appearance and becomes difficult to distinguish from sugar maple, the flaked bark of which it now begins to resemble. The venerable giants on the Bear Mountain Trail in the Cranberry Lake Wild Forest are a striking example of this. Other "virgin" yellow birch may be seen in the Saranac Lake Wild Forest along the shores of Middle Saranac Lake or Round Lake.

Yellow birch saplings frequently light the way of abandoned logging roads languishing deep in the Forest Preserve. This is apparently because their seeds prefer small openings in the forest to germinate and begin their lives. The moss-covered tops of glacial erratics are also suitable in this regard; a common sight is that of a large yellow birch growing atop a boulder with its roots almost completely enveloping it as they grow through the moss down the sides of the boulder to reach the soil of the forest floor.

Never to be forgotten is the occasion when the growth of young yellow birch, along the route of the long-defunct Albany Road deep in the trailless area of the Five Ponds Wilderness, enabled me to find my way back to the lean-to at High Falls just as evening set in. A close call indeed!

Yellow birch rates as top-notch browse for white-tailed deer, especially in winter. Recent studies conducted at the Adirondack Ecological Center in Newcomb disclose, in fact, that deer can completely eliminate yellow birch from the understory of wide areas of the forest. This situation can be seen today in many parts of the Adirondacks.

Winter finches, especially pine siskins, appear to relish the small cones of yellow birch and feed extensively on them during this time of year. Their small seeds strewn on the ground, often from feeding, make quite a splendid sight of brown on white during this season. Porcupines and beavers take delight in the smooth bark of young yellow birch and the marks of their feeding are present through the year. The crotches of the medium-sized trees have harbored at least ninety percent of the broad-winged hawk nests that I have seen in our area.

For me, the stirring sight of these ancient monarchs, slowly withering away in their grandeur, represents the essence of the Adirondack hardwood forest even more than the noble sugar maple.

HEMLOCK

The most ancient of all Adirondack tree specimens has been known to attain ages in excess of five hundred years. The graceful and majestic hemlock is a vital element of the Adirondack ecosystem. It furnishes nutritious browse for white-tailed deer in winter, while at the same time effectively excludes heavy snow and the fatal, bone-numbing winter winds from the "deer yard." Porcupines love to browse on the needles of hemlock at this time of year and often litter the ground under them with boughs that have fallen as a result of their feeding. The deer eagerly accept this "green on white" offering from the tree-tops as a supplement to their browsing. Snowshoe hares browse heavily on the needles and twigs in winter, much as they do with spruce and fir needles. I have been unable to detect a preference from my own observations.

In our area hemlock is amply represented on lake shores and in cool, moist ravines. It also appears to thrive on the gravelly soils of eskers and other glacial outwash forms. It does not ascend as high up the slopes as red spruce or balsam fir, but is fairly common on the lower slopes. In our area of modest mountains they may be found almost up to the tops.

Majestic specimens of mature hemlock may be noted in the Cranberry Lake Wild Forest along the trail to Bear Mountain. Some appear to show signs of weakening, possibly because of the increase in open area and in sunlight created by the demise of many of the ancient beech trees nearby due to the ravages of the beech fungus. Hemlock do not thrive in open areas! A magnificent forty-two-inch Diameter Breast High (DBH) specimen along the Peavine Creek Trail died a mere five years after construction of the trail by the DEC. The slight opening created by the trail played host to increased sunlight and also to an increase in velocity of another culprit—wind.

The apex of old-growth magnificence is reached along the trail to the top of Ampersand Mountain. Here the hemlocks and northern hardwoods are the chief players in producing a true old-growth diamond, sprawling over hundreds of acres. The stillness, enchantment, aura of splendor, yet mystery, prevailing here offer a rare insight into what our woodlands were before the advent of European settlement.

Hemlock appears to be doing just fine in the Adirondacks, although hemlock in the Blue Ridge Mountains of Virginia are being destroyed en masse by the hemlock aldegid, an invertebrate killer that has not yet made its way to these mountains. Even if it does, I have a hunch hemlock will outlast it. The old log roads that lace the forest today give testament to the mass destruction of hemlock around the turn of the century to furnish raw material for the tanning factory that once dominated the hamlet of Fine. Today, hemlock sends its spines to the sky again, while all that remains of the factory are foundation walls!

BALSAM FIR

The ultimate in wild fragrance, the boughs of the Adirondack balsam were the woodland bed of preference for the sportsmen of an earlier era when they had to spend a night under the stars. Balsam is still used extensively for Christmas trees and as a source of stuffing for miniature fragrant "pillows" hawked as curios to eager tourists.

Balsam seeds profusely in small openings in the Adirondack forest, including, quite often, along the sides of old logging roads. It appears to do best in semi-shade rather than full sunlight, although I have seen it seed directly on old hay fields near Star Lake. Often it is allied with red spruce in dominating moderately wet swamps and also can unfailingly be noted along the many languid stretches of boreal river that meander through the region.

Balsam is not nearly as long-lived as red spruce and also is somewhat inferior to it in height. The state-wide champion in height is alleged to be in the Independence River Wild Forest on the southern extremity of the Great South Woods. For years a specimen stood along the trail to Round Lake in the Aldrich Pond Wild Forest that easily rivaled a champion-sized tree farther south. Alas, a windstorm in 1992 completely toppled this tree and deposited its imposing length parallel to the ground!

In the swamps and along rivers balsam appears to be forever toppling over. Its extremely shallow roots and the usually water-logged soils make the tree very vulnerable to being uprooted during periods of heavy wind. This makes these swamps a fantastic place for snowshoe hares, but a distinctly difficult place for humans to progress on foot!

Hares browse extensively on fir needles in winter, as do white-tailed deer. Repeated browsing by deer creates all kinds of contortions in the shape of young balsam, as can be readily seen in the Chandler Pond Wild Forest deer yard near Sevey's Corners, at the junction of Routes 3 and 56. Despite this intensive utilization, balsam browse is apparently only dessert to deer as far as nutrition goes since they can actually die of starvation if the diet of balsam is not supplemented by cedar, hemlock or hardwoods.

The smooth bark of the balsam attracts the black bear to claw and bite, marking its territory. These rectangular gashes made by the bears are frequently noted on balsam trees located on the sides of trails, often near a body of water. Also seen frequently at the base of balsam fir trees are the large rectangular holes made by foraging pileated woodpeckers in search of colonies of luscious carpenter ants hibernating during the long winter months.

Brevity of life-span and all, the Great South Woods would not be the same without the presence of balsam fragrance to lift the spirit.

WHITE BIRCH

The tree most intimately connected with the Native Americans, who dwelt on the periphery of the Adirondacks, is undoubtedly the white birch. This handsome tree was used almost exclusively to furnish the birch bark canoes that originally plied the many waterways of the area.

White birch prefers larger openings than does yellow birch and along with aspen often pioneers after fire and wind-throw. It is nearly always present at the tops of the low mountains of the Great South Woods: Panther, Dog Pond, Azure, Mount Arab, etc. I never fail to find it here, somewhat stunted, as is the red spruce that invariably accompanies it. The incessant winds and the shallow soil the trees root in probably account for this.

White birch is at its best looming above an ice-clad Adirondack pond in winter with its pure chalky white bark highlighted by the lacy green of the white pine that also invariably accompanies it. Like white pine, white birch can be adversely impacted by road salt.

Some of the old-timers in the town of Fine used to tap white birch for their rising sap in spring. For their efforts they received a paltry return when compared to the sugar maple.

Around the winter deer yards, it has been my experience that white birch, while not exactly shunned, are not relished in the same category as certain other hardwoods, including its relative, yellow birch. Still, white birch typically denotes the young forests of the Adirondacks and can invoke stunning memories of other boreal areas of the Northeast. Its absence would leave something of a void in the Great South Woods.

WHITE CEDAR

Is there a tree more intimately associated with the white-tailed deer of the Great South Woods in winter than the white cedar? It is the favorite by far of all the arboreal browse of deer during this season. A look along the shores of Adirondack ponds at any time of the year clearly reveals this. The browse line on the white cedars lining the shores reflects the height that deer standing on the ice can reach.

White cedar grows extensively in certain wooded swamps of the Adirondacks. In our area it is not quite as common as in the vicinity of Newcomb, where I occasionally lead trips at the Adirondack Visitor Interpretive Center. The Grenville limestone bedrock, underlying much of the surface in the Newcomb region, probably accounts for the greater abundance of white cedar here for it is one northern tree that responds positively to soil that is neutral.

Deer do not wait until deep snow cover restricts them to their yards in winter to begin browsing on white cedar. Every few years white cedar saplings grow to a height of approximately two feet on the side of Route 3 in front of my house. As soon as the ground is blanketed with snow, even if only to a depth of an inch or so, the deer make directly for these saplings and happily browse on them until they eliminate them entirely from the site for the next several years.

A white cedar swamp is truly a place of wonder if for no other reason than the rather rare (to the Adirondacks) flora that can be found flourishing there. Particularly in evidence are members of the orchid family, especially the gorgeous, showy lady's slipper which can be found upon occasion. Less common is the ram's head lady's slipper with its more subdued beauty. The entrancing rumors of yellow lady's slipper that frequently surface locally add a spice of intrigue. I have not located it but know those who claim they have. If so, they zealously (or jealously?) guard the exact locale, perhaps rightly so.

The largest white cedar I have seen is in the vicinity of Rich Lake at the Newcomb Visitor Interpretive Center. Here, trees tower almost one hundred feet high and reflect close to two centuries of growing. In our area, only scattered giants on the fringes of Peavine Swamp and other locations in the Cranberry Lake Wild Forest can compare with this.

The white cedar swamp may be fairly rare locally, but nonetheless, is an integral component of the Great South Woods.

TAMARACK

Tamarack, also known as larch, has two main claims to fame in the Great South Woods. It is the only conifer to shed its leaves in autumn. It is also perhaps the stellar candidate for the title of most boreal tree in the Adirondack Park.

Tamarack grows only in the cold, austere peatlands and on the sandy and gravelly glacial knolls and plains laid down by the Ice Age. Its hand is still readily apparent on all sides in the Great South Woods. In the peatlands, tamarack has as its partner black spruce, while on the glacial outwash it is accompanied by white pine, hemlock, and red spruce.

Tamarack needs sunlight, but can grow fairly rapidly and attain a respectable size. A common sight is that of tamarack towering over black spruce as the two of them surround one of the numerous minia-ture peatlands and tiny ponds in the Cranberry Lake Wild Forest. Tamarack is also common on the sandy soils of the Chandler Pond Wild Forest near Sevey's Corners. This wild forest and adjacent private lands host one of the largest deer yards in the entire Adirondack Park, yet the deer seem to browse only infrequently on the buds and twigs of the tamarack in winter. The usnea "moss" (actually a lichen) so con-spicuous here, hanging from the branches of the tamarack, receives somewhat more attention from the white-tailed deer. I often speculate on the caribou that probably lived here until the beginning of the his-toric area, and how they would have found the usnea a veritable manna in the desert. More's the pity they're not still around.

The mature tamarack that grew early in the century on the edge of the Oswegatchie Plains was heavily decimated by the larch sawfly. Some of the snags may still be seen standing today. Aside from this ap-parent local infestation, however, the tamarack in the area appears to be thriving.

One final thrust in late October might possibly be said to define the visual role of the tamarack in the Adirondacks best of all. Several weeks after the hardwood leaves have fallen to the forest floor, the leaves of the tamarack turn a glorious golden yellow that positively lights up the otherwise somber forest. Although this gorgeous coloration is only a prelude to the leaves dropping, it is just cause to celebrate the tamarack's place in the Adirondack forest. This alone would provide reasons galore to lament the disappearance of the tamarack from the Great South Woods.

BLACK CHERRY

An Adirondack surprise: a tree not generally present in the other boreal forests of the Northeast, black cherry is fairly common in the forests of the western Adirondacks. I clearly remember the surprise registered by a forester who had recently transferred from Nova Scotia to the Newton Falls Paper Company when he first noted the presence of black cherry here. The forester, a native of Maine, was on a trip I was leading and could not believe the relative prevalence of cherry here as opposed to in his former area of employment.

From my observations, a wide disparity exists in the quality of black cherry in our area. The cherry so common in the Aldrich Pond Wild Forest near Streeter Lake appears of poor form and also seems to be continually susceptible to wind-throw. In the Cranberry Lake Wild Forest, west of Streeter, can be found truly awesome, relatively straight-growing cherry that resembles those of the Catskills and Pennsylvania. I am at a loss to explain the difference, although some of it may result from differences in soil composition and, perhaps, varying levels of acid precipitation. In both areas, frost scars are common on the trees, as are signs of the black knot fungus. In recent years, owners of private woodlands locally have received a bonanza in the price paid for their black cherry by the Ethan Allen Furniture Company of Connecticut, which has been seeking out cherry in this region to replace the depleted stocks farther south.

No matter what the form or stature, another fact has become irrefutably clear to me: black cherry is by far the leading producer of soft mast in the Adirondacks! From late August through early November, most of the trails in our area are littered not only with the dark fruit of the cherry, but also with tangible signs left by the forest's wildlife citizens when feeding on the fruit. Scat—everywhere—from fox, raccoon, coyote, black bear—is a continual testament to their walking the trails, mostly in the dark, and gorging as they trek along! The fruits along the trail are much easier for the gorgers to discern—at least before leaf fall.

In addition to the above, fisher, grouse, chipmunks, red squirrels, and deer mice, among others, are known to feed extensively on black cherry fruit. Black bears often do not wait for the fruit to fall; they frequently climb the trees to secure their harvest. The marks they leave are not as noticeable as those left in ascending the smooth-barked beech, but still can be detected. The gnarled black cherry invading the Oswegatchie Plains bears witness to their feeding through both the reddish inner bark uncovered in climbing and the twisted branches left by the ravenous bruins in getting at the fruit.

If only for this wildlife dimension alone, black cherry has assumed an importance in the Great South Woods out of all proportion to its actual numbers!

WHITE ASH and BASSWOOD

Frequently growing together, white ash and basswood are a minor but regular component of the Adirondack forest in our area. Wherever they appear, they indicate some of the richest forest soils in the Great South Woods. Invariably I come upon some of the most haunting woodland wildflowers, often spring ephemerals, growing around their trunks: wild leek, blue cohosh, hepatica, dicentra (both squirrel corn and Dutchmen's breeches) and occasionally, even those most delicate of blooms, bloodroot and wild ginger. Especially if basswood is present, most of these will always be found. Add to this the rare presence of the magical ginseng and it is obvious why basswood and white ash groves are truly places of enchantment.

White ash is the last Adirondack hardwood tree to leaf out in spring. Often I have noticed this does not occur completely until the last week in May. This fact and the long vertical "frost" scars often noted on ash are indicators that they are only marginally suited to the cold Adirondack climate.

Basswood often grows from sprouts in the northwest Adirondacks. Although there appears to be adequate seed production (I have noticed deer mice hoarding the seeds in autumn), from my observations it appears that most reproduction might come from these sprouts. Basswood appears to like growing along streams and at the base of cliffs, although I have found colonies on knolls several miles from the nearest road deep in the Five Ponds Wilderness near Star Lake. White ash, for its part, appears to be generally more scattered through the forest, with the finest examples I have seen occurring in the old-growth hardwoods of the Five Ponds Wilderness. Here trees grow one hundred feet tall, straight as an arrow with DBH of only two feet or so—wood fit for the making of Louisville Sluggers mighty enough for the likes of a Babe Ruth!

Deer do not appear to browse extensively on either white ash or basswood, at least not from my observations. Possibly this is due only to the relative rarity of the trees and nothing more. There is no doubt, however, that the tender buds and leaves of basswood are especially beloved of porcupines during the summer. How often have I looked upward and seen a porcupine reposing in the upper branches at this time of year. For white ash, the image that springs most readily to mind is that of swirling flocks of evening grosbeaks alighting on the tree branches in winter to feed on the bounteous supply of seeds present during this season.

Infrequent lovers of fertile soil, the white ash and basswood add both variety and a little glamour to the Adirondack forest.

ASPEN

A constant companion of white birch in the pioneering of open terrain in the Adirondacks, quaking aspen has achieved note of late with the revelation that certain stands are among the oldest organisms in the world! Aspen often reproduces from sprouts, as can readily be observed in the Great South Woods in any open field returning to forest. Recent studies in Colorado have disclosed that some of these "clone" forests are thousands of years old, making them the oldest known living entities with the possible exception of certain fungi.

While Aspen is usually found with white birch, I have noted subtle differences between the two with either one or the other showing more vigorous growth under certain conditions. Bare gravelly soil, for instance, seems to be ideal for aspen to germinate and start the march back to a forest. This can be clearly seen in the disturbed soil along state highways (Route 30 between Tupper Lake and Long Lake springs readily to mind) and also in the sterile moss-cushioned soil in the old Shuler Potato Patch in the Aldrich Pond Wild Forest. Quaking aspen, like white birch, is relatively short-lived, with most trees dead within a century. The closely related big tooth aspen, which flowers two weeks later in the spring, can grow somewhat older and also a bit larger. I often see the two species growing in close contact with each other.

Many Adirondack wildlife species seem to have a special affinity for aspen. I often see grouse feeding on their catkins in early spring. It has long been local lore that beaver prefer the bark of aspen to all other woody browse, while sapsuckers seek the vicinity of groves of aspen to nest in late spring. Deer appear to browse aspen only moderately in winter, but I received a surprise in the mid-1980s when I found the extensive stands of aspen on the edge of the Oswegatchie Plain had been heavily browsed by a much mightier herbivore than the white-tailed deer—his majesty the moose. Moose prefer aspen along with balsam and striped maple for their winter browse. After a bout of feeding, the stand looks almost decimated but inevitably returns to normal. Moose also bite into the bark of aspen, leaving tooth marks for posterity. I discovered this one day while snowshoeing through the Horseshoe Lake Wild Forest.

Aspen is a unique tree and it is quite fitting that the ancient bedrock of the Adirondacks has some equally ancient trees growing on top of it!

RED PINE and SCOTCH PINE

Two trees of strikingly colored bark but with a markedly different background, red pine and Scotch pine, seem to be linked together in the Great South Woods. Red pine is a rare native while Scotch pine is an exotic. They both, however, have been widely established in conifer plantations throughout the region.

Scotch pine is one of the few non-native trees to be established on its own as part of the Adirondack flora. The sight of their handsome orange bark, deep in what today are secluded parts of the Forest Preserve, never ceases to amaze me. I think particularly of plantations in the Five Ponds Wilderness several miles upriver from Inlet and of another one located in the Aldrich Pond Wild Forest midway between Star Lake and Streeter Lake. Reproduction also occurs at least sporadically in these cases—I know of a beaver wetland on the New York State Ranger School lands at Wanakena where all the upland fringes have been extensively colonized by Scotch pine saplings.

Unlike most conifers, Scotch pine appears to be uniquely favored by certain native wildlife. Deer relish the buds and twigs in winter; perhaps it is only stuffing food like balsam fir, but it is nonetheless widely utilized by them during this season, according to my observations. Hare also browse it in winter, as they do other pines, but it is when we come to beaver and porcupine that we see really intensive use of this tree. The bark of Scotch pine appears to extend an overwhelming attraction for these two large rodents in winter. Porcupine browse on the bark high up, while beaver attack at the base of the tree. Beaver utilize the bark of Scotch pine as food (as opposed to cutting the tree to use in erecting dams and lodges) far more that they use the bark of any native conifer.

Red pine is found only in a few select locations, principally areas where competition from hardwoods is less intense. These may include windy peninsulas on large lakes and the gravelly soils of eskers and other glacial land forms. In St. Lawrence County I have found them in several places along the shores of Cranberry Lake and Big Tupper Lake as well as on the eskers separating Massawepie Lake, Boot Tree Pond, Horseshoe Pond, and others on the Massawepie Boy Scout property.

These native stands of red pine are generally quite open and have a diverse floral understory. I often find pipsissewa, arbutus, sheep laurel, and other boreal rarities underneath them, as well as the more widespread shadbush, hazelnut, and others. The red pine stands established in the Chandler Pond Wild Forest by Bernhard Fernow, the father of American forestry, have such a lush undergrowth of balsam fir saplings that they are heavily used by deer as browse in that expansive winter deer yard.

Red pine appear not to have the appeal of Scotch pine as a browse favorite for deer and beaver in winter. This is definitely not the case as far as snowshoe hare are concerned. My own ten-acre red pine stand, planted in 1974, began to be utilized by hares in 1985 and use increased until around 1993, when it began to decline. The red pine stand, however, continued to be the favorite nighttime summer roost of the mourning doves who had recently expanded their range to our area, probably because of the mild winters during the 1980s.

These two closely related species, while not a major component of our forest, now are an integral part of its overall arboreal diversity.

RED MAPLE

Here is a tree that truly is a little bit everywhere in the Great South Woods. Swamps, abandoned fields, spruce flats, hillsides, all contain their small share of red maple, but nowhere does it dominate. Often overlooked, in part because it pales in comparison with its more glamorous cousin, the sugar maple, it still manages to survive and thrive.

The red maple does give some maple syrup but its output is overshadowed by that of the sugar maple. It does not grow to either the majestic proportions or ancient age of the sugar maple, yet I have seen occasional specimens in the Aldrich Pond Wild Forest that approached one hundred feet in height.

Red maple buds burst into flower in early spring, giving a decidedly reddish tint to many an Adirondack hillside. The fruits, called keys, also appear early and furnish food to a variety of wildlife, especially chipmunks, whom I have watched gorge themselves on the fallen fruit that litters the forest floor in late spring.

It is, however, as a top-quality deer browse that red maple achieves its primary importance to wildlife. Unlike the sugar maple and yellow birch, which are oft eliminated from the forest understory, the red maple assumes the shape of a hedge and endures persistent winter deer browse year after year. These odd-shaped trees are much in evidence in the Chandler Pond Wild Forest deer yard.

All in all, a small but significant part of the Great South Woods!

SUGAR MAPLE

Two regal monarchs vie in popular acclaim for the title "emperor of the Adirondack forest." The sugar maple is one of these and is generally accorded "pride of place" among the hardwoods. What indeed can be more enticing or memory-producing than a mellow early spring day spent in the sunshine of a sugarbush, while the flowing sap pours forth from the lords of that bush?

A good deal of maple syrup is still produced locally, although some of it is shipped to Vermont and marketed there as "Vermont maple syrup." Some of the finest syrup, made with the latest state-of-the-art equipment and tubing, is to be found in the western Adirondack region. I think, specifically, of the impressive sugarbushes in the town of Croghan on the road to the Watson's East Wild Forest.

Sugar maple usually occupies rich soil areas. I have never found it growing on glacial eskers or similar geologic sites. The rare (for the Adirondacks) basswood and white ash sometimes accompany it, as does the full spectrum of woodland spring herbs and ephemerals.

Sugar maple can attain an age of four hundred years, probably the maximum for the Adirondack hardwood. Trees this ancient can be observed on the trail to Ampersand Mountain in the High Peaks Wilderness Area, as well as in the vicinity of Griffin Rapids in the Five Ponds Wilderness area. Both are areas of true old growth. Another locale harboring ancient monarchs is Bear Mountain in the Cranberry Lake Wild Forest. Trees can be seen on the trail from the campsite and present a truly imposing spectacle despite the fact that the forest does not qualify for old growth status due to the sporadic logging of conifers done over a century ago.

Adirondack sugar maples appear healthy, although a possible hazard might loom on the horizon in the form of the pear thrips, an insect which has already caused damage in Quebec and Vermont.

Many of the ancient monarchs have a hoary aspect to them, usually denoting hollow areas in the still-live tree. This is perhaps one of the main benefits to wildlife furnished by this tree in the Adirondacks. The only pine marten I have seen exiting from a tree den was one that came forth from a large hole part way up a sugar maple snag. Sugar maple is also heavily browsed by white-tailed deer. This browsing curtails regrowth of the shade-loving species making it sparse in the undergrowth of some mature forests where it should be much more in evidence.

A fitting emblem, when all is said, as the official tree of the state of New York!

WHITE PINE

The other contender for the appellation "emperor of the Adirondack forest" is the equally regal white pine. The tallest by far of any Adirondack tree, the white pine occasionally reaches heights to rival the fabled coastal redwoods of California. It is as clearly the king of the conifers as the sugar maple is lord of the hardwoods.

Although white pine purportedly reached heights in excess of two hundred feet in the colonial Adirondack landscape, the tallest I have seen are around 170 feet. Trees of this size are between four hundred and five hundred years old and are exceeded in age only by hemlock in the Great South Woods. Possibly the best area for viewing trees of this magnitude is in the aptly named Pine Ridge on the upper Oswegatchie south of High Falls. Individual record-breaking white pine are scattered south of the hamlet of Wanakena where they protrude above and totally eclipse the canopy of spruce and northern hardwood nestled beneath them. This effect of pine towering above a mature canopy can also be seen in the Cranberry Lake Wild Forest along Route 3, east of the hamlet of Cranberry Lake.

Several decades ago, white pine was threatened by blister rust—a fungus which utilized wild currants as an alternate host. Manual eradication of wild currants in the vicinity of large stands of white pine considerably mitigated this threat. Of late, the pine false wellworm is making inroads on forests in St. Lawrence County immediately north of the Adirondack Park. This sawfly might present a future problem.

White pine also appears highly susceptible to road salt. The toppling over of an 80-foot specimen in front of my house attests quite definitely to this fact. With white pine seeding prolifically every four or five years and the seeds being broadcast for up to a mile, there probably is no need to worry about regeneration of white pine in the Adirondacks. All that's needed is sufficient open areas, preferably on glacial ridges or on sandy outwash plains.

White pine is frequently seen on the banks of the region's boreal rivers as they meander on their way to the St. Lawrence. I have seen nests of both Cooper's hawks and red-shouldered hawks in these situations. Mourning doves, too, seem to prefer white pine to place their flimsy nests. These are increasing in the peripheral areas of the western

Adirondacks. As for mammals, there can be no denying the attraction that young, smooth-barked white pine has for porcupines, especially in winter. Porcupines are a significant source of mortality on young white pine in our Adirondack forest!

Long may this noble giant wave over the Great South Woods.

BEECH

According to a long-hallowed Adirondack tradition, beech is the prime producer of mast for wildlife in these woods. I generally concur, although from my observations black cherry is a more reliable year-by-year producer, of soft mast at least. Beech has a tendency to produce an abundant nut crop after a year or two of rather poor crops, but is still unrivaled as far as hard mast is concerned.

Soft mast or hard mast, the indisputable fact remains that beechnuts are beloved by a wide array of creatures spanning a broad spectrum of Adirondack wildlife. From the chipmunks that gorge themselves on an October ridge top in preparation for winter hibernation, to the bears and raccoons that likewise gorge themselves for more or less the same reason, the beech tree appears to be indispensable to the local fauna. Add to that the fox, coyote, and fisher which supplement their usual fare of flesh with beechnuts, and the avian lovers of this tender morsel—grouse, turkey, blue jays, even ravens, and it is readily apparent that wildlife could be in trouble in the Great South Woods without them!

That trouble could have already appeared. Older beech in the area are currently being ravaged by a disease resulting from a combination of a scale insect and a fungus acting in inadvertent tandem to decimate most stands. The disease's progress has been uneven so far, with trees in the Adirondacks receiving more damage than trees in the St. Lawrence Valley, where growing conditions are more hospitable. The contrast is evident when viewing the massive destruction of the old-growth beech on the slopes of Ampersand and Bear Mountains and then comparing it to the relatively moderate damage incurred by the beech growing at Indian Creek Nature Center near Canton. I feel the more optimal growing conditions in the valley give the trees greater buffering strength against the disease.

Even before the advent of this disease, beech appeared to be much healthier in the valley than in the Adirondacks. Beech is, along with white ash, the last hardwood tree to unfurl its leaves in the spring. Add to that the frequent frost scars evident on mature beech, and it becomes readily apparent that beech is a tree whose colonization of the higher-elevation Adirondack sites has been quite tenuous in many areas.

Whither go the beech and wildlife if this carnage continues unabated? There is no lack of beech replenishment so far in the Adirondacks. As beech frequently sprout from roots of older trees, a common sight in winter is of hordes of beech saplings, with their dead brown leaves still clinging to them, monopolizing the forest understory beneath a canopy of their dead and dying ancestors. Will this suffice to fuel the larder of wildlife that depend on beechnuts to carry them through the winter? The bear, whose "nests" in the trees are readily visible through the winter following a peak mast year—what will happen to its numbers if it is not able to adapt? Not to mention the goshawk, which, from my observations, seems to be restricted to beech trees for constructing their bulky nests in early spring? Even the beaver prefers the thin bark of beech for browse, though often it is unattainable because of its habit of growing on hillsides. Woodsmen firmly state that beech is the only tree that will not be readily struck by lightning. My observations confirm this. Where will the sojourner stranded in the forest during a sudden summer electric storm seek shelter if there are no mature beech?

For the sake of the creatures of the Great South Woods we can only fervently pray that the disease run its course or that the next generation of beech is able to build up a resistance to this relentless ravager.

SOME TREES ON THE EDGE

A number of miscellaneous tree species seem, in many respects, to be marginal in the Great South Woods. This marginality may occur because of their rarity in the forest or because of stunted size or generally poor form. A number of them are listed below. Black spruce is a little more typical of the area and perhaps deserves mention in its own right, but I have arbitrarily elected to list it here. A change in climate and conditions could have the effect of eliminating some of these trees from our flora or, conversely, could allow some of them to increase markedly in abundance.

RED OAK

I come across red oak scattered sparingly throughout the town of Fine, up to an altitude of 1,100 feet. Wherever the oak is, gray squirrels seem to be trying to establish an Adirondack beach head. A few impressive trees are located in the Aldrich Pond Wild Forest in the vicinity of the abandoned hamlet of Kalurah. I have also seen some splendid specimens of this species near Blue Mountain Lake. But in between is a vast void where red oak has apparently been unable to establish itself.

According to foresters, red oak's inability to survive over most of the Adirondacks is due to the fact they are unable to tolerate temperature extremes of below -40° during winter. Temperatures beneath this level freeze the cambium layer and the tree succumbs.

On my land, oak saplings and young trees are common around the house—usually under a sheltering shrub or tree. They arrived here and sprouted courtesy of blue jays, which transported the acorns from the forest interior several hundred yards away and then buried them for future use, as is the way of the jay. For one reason or another, the jays never uncovered them and so the acorns sprouted. What fate awaits these juvenile oaks will be revealed in the future.

BLACK SPRUCE

Usually found growing under a canopy of tamarack in the area's peatlands, black spruce can also be found growing locally in some of the extensive sandy outwash terraces that dot the region. In one of them, the fabled Oswegatchie Plains, the tree has made widespread use of "layering" as a means of regeneration. Wherever it is, black spruce never attains great stature and, invariably, seems to have small cones. In a few tiny peatlands that surround open ponds, black spruce appears to have hybridized with red spruce. Several of these "dimpled jewels" are located in the Cranberry Lake Wild Forest just east of the hamlet of Cranberry Lake.

Black spruce seems to be a necessary ingredient for the presence of the endangered spruce grouse in our area. The tree appears crucial in this regard, possibly in combination with balsam fir. The constant presence of cones on black spruce also assures that they are a favorite of certain "winter finches." I often note flocks near their vicinity in winter—all in all, another element to enhance the boreal enchantment of the Great South Woods!

MOUNTAIN ASH

The blazing of the crests of the area's low mountains, beginning in October, signifies the ripening of the scarlet fruit of the mountain ash. This rather modest tree, which also grows sparingly through the local spruce swamps, provides some vital supplemental nutrition at this time of the year to an assorted variety of wildlife.

Flocks of robins and evening grosbeaks positively gorge on the fruit, the former to increase reserves of fat crucial for their long-distance migration, the latter to obtain nourishment to survive a North Country winter.

Fisher and marten appear to have evolved in a manner that enables them to utilize these berries—often they are the only mast available in the deep woods at this time of year. I have seen a number of instances where fisher fed on the fruit in winter, both on top and in the spruce swamps.

Quite unexpected was the heavy feeding on the fruit I encountered one time from a source that, to me at least, was a surprise. It occurred as follows: I had planted two pairs each of mountain ash and its close relative, the European rowan tree, in back of my house approximately a decade before the incident. Sentiment played a part in the planting; the rowan tree was considered sacred to my Druid ancestors.

One January morning I went outside and found deer had been feeding heavily on the berries, so much so that they had broken a number of them. This has been repeated several winters since then—the deer feeding vigorously on the fruit and only incidentally on the buds of the mountain ash.

These Great South Woods would be definitely diminished without that dash of ridge-top "fire" in autumn!

BLACK ASH

A pale imitation of its close relative white ash, I find black ash growing as stragglers in some of the area's swamps. A swamp forest with red maple, from my experience, is more likely to harbor black ash, although occasionally it can be encountered in the more boreal swamps.

Wherever it grows, black ash does not appear to be thriving. Many of the trees have a poor form and seem to be struggling to survive. Whether this is due to disease or insect damage or is just their natural appearance, I am uncertain.

Black ash attracts flocks of evening grosbeaks like white ash, although it does not appear to fruit as heavily. I think I have noted heavy browsing, by white-tailed deer in winter, of the bud and twigs of black ash. This could be because of the tendency of black ash to grow in the vicinity of winter deer yards.

I know of a few old-timers in the Great South Woods who still utilize black ash in making Adirondack pack baskets, as do some Native Americans on the Mohawk reservation near Hogansburg. Aside from this, I have to be candid and state that the disappearance of black ash from the local flora would be missed only for the resulting decrease in biodiversity.

X

WEATHER PHENOMENA

Photo by Gerry Lemmo

Trees blown by high winds

Adirondack legend has traditionally proclaimed that a violent windstorm of landscape-altering proportions will descend on the area once every century. The rather sparse literature available on the subject seems to support this. Still, most were unprepared for what transpired in the wee hours of the morning of July 15, 1995. An intense storm of a magnitude unprecedented in local memory roared through St. Lawrence County, leaving a path of destruction and devastation in its wake.

The storm in many aspects was a classic microburst, a mass of cool Canadian air arriving rapidly on the scene and lifting the warm humid air, in place, to heights where it cooled rapidly and unleashed precipitation along with large hailstones and winds of up to eighty miles per hour in some areas. The storm was quite selective, striking areas in a haphazard and sporadic fashion. Harrisville was hard-hit while Fine was mostly bypassed, as was Cranberry Lake. Wanakena and Star Lake received the full brunt of the storm, with portions of the latter practically decimated. The storm then roared through the Forest Preserve south of the two hamlets, causing severe damage to large areas of the forest.

High Falls, the west end of Lows Lake, and the Five Ponds Esker were among the areas familiar to regional outdoorsmen that were heavily impacted. Trees lay across each other in every possible direction as whole swaths of forest were denuded of all medium and large trees. An occasional one fell unimpeded to lie prone on the ground, but this was generally rare because of the thoroughness of the destruction in several areas. A preliminary assessment put the total area of impact at 60,000 acres with about half the total acreage being essentially blown over completely. A considerable and as yet undetermined portion of this area of impact consisted of authentic old-growth forest. Majestic white pine was snapped off at the bole by the force of the wind, as was the equally deep-rooted aspen. More shallow-rooted spruce and fir were blown entirely over, leaving gaping holes where their roots previously were. Even sugar maple and yellow birch, normally fairly resistant to wind-throw, were tumbled over like matchsticks in the path of the zephyr. Pine plantations and other monocultures appeared to be especially susceptible. The wind seemed to be especially powerful along rivers and lake shores and on the tops of eskers, causing considerable mortality in these places.

Occasionally, in the past, storms of great magnitude have also occurred, leveling large areas of the forest. This happened in the blowdown of November 1950 and before that in a tornado that leveled a swath of land through the entire county in 1845. The latter, known as the "windfall," is commemorated locally today by a brook, a restaurant and a hunting club. Extensive fires also leveled large areas of forest in 1903 and 1908. These fires, however, were anthropocentric in origin, being ignited by sparks from locomotives of the logging railroads so common at that time. Extensive disturbance therefore appears to be not only an integral part of the ecosystem process but also to be primarily initiated in our area by severe windstorm rather than by fire.

The two, previous large-scale wind disturbances differed from the blowdown of 1995 in both origin and scale. The blowdown of 1950 was a classic Northeaster which arrived in November after the hardwood trees had shed their leaves. It encompassed a wider area of destruction than the microburst but in general was more local in the havoc it wrought. At the time, the New York Attorney General rendered an ill-conceived judicial decision that damaged and downed trees in the Forest Preserve could be harvested. The log roads that resulted from this salvage harvest wind their way ever-sketchily through remote areas of today's forest as a reminder of this calamity of half a century ago. Some of the larger fallen trees of that time also remain prone on the floor of the preserve, often impeding the progress of woodland travelers. This is particularly in evidence on the slopes of the Seward Range where these fallen giants are still encountered by aspiring 46ers making their way up the trailless slopes.

A veritable explosion of the white-tailed deer population occurred in the aftermath of the 1950 storm. This upward spiral in deer numbers lasted for approximately two decades and, according to local woodsmen, ceased only upon the advent of a doe season in the Adirondacks. It differed also from the latest blowdown in that extensive areas of the Forest Preserve were declared off-limits to human intrusion for a number of years after the storm. This practice was not followed after the 1995 microburst.

The windfall of 1845, on the other hand, resembled a tornado in many respects. It leveled a wide swath of land in St. Lawrence County from Fowler, through Edwards, and on to Cranberry Lake. For a number of years afterwards it spurred modest development locally as the fallen trees were quickly removed and a form of subsistence agriculture was inaugurated in the newly-cleared areas. The settlers who came usually lasted a generation or so at most as the land was inherently unsuitable for agriculture due to constraints of weather and soil. The path of destruction of this storm can still be glimpsed today, albeit vaguely. One area where the forest shows evidence of the windfall is located on the leased timberlands of the John Hancock Insurance Company in the town of Clifton.

What does all this augur for the Adirondack ecosystem in general and for Adirondack wildlife in particular? Fire and wind-throw and the subsequent reversion of a forest to an earlier pioneer stage appear to be a regular component of ecosystem processes. This is attested to by the prevailing patch-gap pattern of existing Adirondack old growth.

The brunt of the damage from the drastic ice storm that struck the North Country in 1998 was restricted to the St. Lawrence Valley. Only some peripheral areas of the Great South Woods in the vicinity of Lampson Falls and Harper Falls received any significant impact from the storm. Such is the unpredictability of weather that, while ice was plaguing the residents of the valley, rain was the order of the day in the normally colder, higher areas of the Great South Woods.

The 1995 storm, while not nearly as widespread as the hurricane of 1950, was much more concentrated. The Great South Woods received the leading edge of that fury. Its effects on individual wildlife species will be mixed, with some gaining and some losing. For now, there are too many imponderables and variables to offer predictions on all species. Still, some trends are readily apparent.

The bird life that favors mature forest will generally decrease in the area, while those that favor openings in the forest canopy should increase their numbers. There already are fewer ovenbirds, red-eyed vireos, solitary vireos, black-throated blue warblers, etc. and a lot more chestnut-sided warblers, mourning warblers and Nashville warblers among others. The resulting buildup in bark beetles and carpenter ants bodes well for all woodpecker species, including the striking pileated and the area's two unique boreal species, the black-backed and three-toed. At least they will wax merrily until the trees devastated by the storm begin to decay.

For Adirondack raptors the future is not quite so clear-cut. Most populations will probably remain stable. The red-tailed hawk, which delights in large openings in the forest, may find conditions more to its liking, while the goshawk, which favors a closed canopy, may not do as well.

The newly-created open areas could provide the boost that the golden eagle requires in its efforts to rekindle a breeding population in the Great South Woods. Prey should not only be more abundant but also considerably easier to hunt.

A study is currently under way to determine the feasibility of restoring elk to the North Country. The openings and semi-openings could enhance foraging opportunities considerably for elk and just may be the factor that tips the balance in their favor.

Moving on to the Adirondacks' favorite cervid, talk is already rife in the area among local wildlife biologists of an impending explosion in the population of white-tailed deer. Severe winters the next decade or two may somewhat hinder this population explosion. However, there is little doubt that deer numbers will ultimately increase in the area. One thing has already been proved to my satisfaction: the jumbled, cluttered mass of downed trees defining the area of blowdown are not going to interfere in the least with the physical passage of deer. I've already observed them on several occasions running at near-full speed through the tangle of trees, with no more sense of hindrance than if they were frolicking through an open meadow.

So too will numbers of snowshoe hares, the area's main middle-sized prey species, increase substantially. Hares have already colonized an area of blowdown where they were totally absent prior to the storm. This area, covering over a hundred acres, consists of pole-sized black cherry and red maple lying strewn across the terrain. Several microtines will also increase in number, among them the red-backed vole and probably the meadow vole.

Concurrent with this increase in prey species will be a corresponding increase in the numbers of most area predators. Fisher and bobcat definitely will profit from the windstorm both in increased prey available and in the increase in snags and downed logs for dens and shelter. Bobcat have in fact begun to respond dramatically to the altered state of the landscape in at least one area. Just outside the hamlet of Wanakena, in a severely-impacted area of hardwood blowdown, I have noted paired bobcat tracks in the snow for the past two spring seasons. The tracks are mainly confined to the nearly impenetrable blowdown area which now furnishes the optimum in security and denning sites. As bobcats are notoriously solitary except while breeding in the spring, this sign seems to indicate breeding at the edge of a hamlet.

Less clear is the impact on the marten. They will benefit from the increase in prey and in dens, but the decrease in standing mature timber could possibly offset this benefit.

The situation with black bears is clear; it is one of paradise found. More food in the form of nutritious berries (raspberries, shadberries, and possibly black cherry) will become almost immediately available. Winter hibernation sites for black bear will also increase markedly.

The prediction for moose is also less clear at this time. There will be a definite increase in the supply of forage for moose but this benefit may be nullified to a degree by an explosion in the deer population. There is evidence that excessive white-tailed deer populations limit moose population, although not as much as believed a decade ago. My feeling is that moose will benefit from the holocaust. Coyote numbers and fox numbers should remain fairly stable.

When it comes to larger predators, they too should definitely benefit ultimately. However, I keep in mind the conversation I once had with the dean of Adirondack wildlife biologists, the wonderfully named Greenleaf Chase. Greenleaf, who unfortunately recently expired while leading a Forest Preserve hiking foray in his mid-80s, told me once that he followed cougar tracks in the 1940s near Saranac Lake. After the 1950 hurricane he expected that cougar numbers would rise dramatically. This was not the case, at least in the number of reported sightings, which stayed approximately the same for the next two decades as they had before the hurricane.

For a true and complete inventory of what will arise we'll have to wait for several decades; such are the variables that can intervene. The only surety that can be predicted is change itself; change in both ecosystem and wildlife numbers will definitely come as a result of this dramatic storm.

Weather is one of the prime factors in the march of life in the Great South Woods. Snow and cold, along with the ice that accompanies them, are almost as predictable as the winter solstice. I have personally witnessed it snowing in every month except July. Up until the past few seasons the snow would remain on the ground for at least five months. Individual storms of three feet or more were virtually guaranteed every winter. The simple fact of this snowfall, along with the record Arctic lows that persist in winter, have interesting ramifications with regard to local fauna. Wildlife must adapt to these extreme conditions, or perish.

The myriad ways in which various members of local fauna adapt, and even thrive, in this time of want, furnish me with a never-ending sense of wonder. White-tailed deer, as noted in previously, have their conifer heaven to which they retreat for protection from cold and snow. Certain species of bats, since they possess the gift of flight, are able to flee far beyond this realm.

Then there are the hibernators. Some like black bears and raccoons are more aptly termed semi-hibernators. They are abroad during warm spells in winter. Others, such as woodchucks, jumping mice, and chipmunks, go into a deep torpor-true hibernation. Chipmunks will stay out, however, as long as they can harvest beechnuts on an autumn ridge. There are also certain species of bats (little brown bats and pipistrelles, for example) that hibernate locally instead of migrating. Their choice of abode is usually a cave or an abandoned mine.

Finally there are those creatures that directly confront the winter scene by making actual, physical adaptations to aid in their survival. Canada lynx, snowshoe hare, and ruffed grouse grow projections and hair on their feet in winter to facilitate movement over snow. Voles and shrews find sustenance and safety, and thrive under the snowy surface during this season. They have the utmost in security except for the persistent weasel that incessantly pursues them through their snowy corridors.

The melting of the snow pack and the warmth of the spring sun's rays spark the forest to life in a coordinated weather-related fashion. First come the flowers of May, those spring ephemerals whose gorgeous subtle blossoms must bloom before the forest leaves unfurl to block out the life-sustaining effects of the sun. Along with these flowers, seemingly magically appear their pollinators, solitary bees of the *andrenid* and *halictid* groups which are attracted to the abundant nectar. Bumble bees and several species of early spring butterflies complete the picture.

When the trees do ultimately leaf out, a host of caterpillars instantly make an appearance and begin to devour the leaves. These ravenous hordes, if allowed to remain unchecked, would swiftly decimate the year's supply of leaves and lead ultimately to the death of the trees. Relief invariably comes, however, with the return of the spring warblers and other songbirds from their winter homes. Caterpillars were clearly put there explicitly for them—a perfect example of weather and wildlife coordination!

I see several rainbows, including the occasional double one, annually. While this weather phenomenon may not provide any direct tangible benefits to the local fauna, it definitely provides an uplift for my spirits. Also in this category is the splendid spectacle of the aurora borealis usually glimpsed in March. The rainbows and the aurora borealis are as much a tonic for the souls of Great South Woods residents as the abundant nitrogen-laden snow is a natural boost to the soil of local vegetable gardeners.

Weather has been a force of reckoning in the Great South Woods since time began. While this may change through global warming, I suspect that Adirondack weather will remain a powerful force in the future.

XI

THE BOB MARSHALL WILDERNESS

Lake Lila

A wilderness, a romantic concept, the dream of a visionary; all this and more can be said of the proposed Bob Marshall Wilderness. The existing Five Ponds Wilderness would be the core of this projected premier eastern one; the proposal also encompasses adjacent public and private wildlands as well.

Beyond a doubt stands the undeniable fact that it contains the largest tract of old-growth forest, as well as the largest area devoid entirely of trails, in the state of New York and quite possibly in the entire eastern part of the United States. It is perhaps the sole area in this long-settled part of our country where extensive biological processes may proceed unimpeded by the hand of man and where a sense of wonder and awe is ever-present concerning what mystery may still remain locked in the fastness of the forest.

It is an area that has completely filled my cup of joy as I have become acquainted with its many wonders and gradually acquired a deeper appreciation of what they truly signify. Although some of the wonders do border on the spectacular, for the most part it is the intricate subtleties and untamed sense of wildness of the area that make it unique and define its very essence.

The visionary was the legendary Bob Marshall, who went on from a summer spent at the New York State Ranger School on Cranberry Lake in the 1920s, to become the foremost proponent of the wilderness ethos nationwide. The largest designated wilderness area in the U.S., the Bob Marshall in Montana, is named in his memory.

In 1936 Bob Marshall drew up a list of all the remaining roadless areas then in existence in the country. The list was formulated in the hope of assuring the ultimate protection of all the areas surveyed. The premier listing for the whole eastern part of the country was that area lying generally north of Stillwater Reservoir and Raquette Lake and south of Cranberry Lake. Bob Marshall was intimately acquainted with this region from his student days at the ranger school. Today, portions of this area are contained in the Five Ponds, Pepperbox, and Pigeon Lake Wilderness Areas as well as in several adjoining Wild Forests. Key private parcels remain mostly in large private parks and corporate timberlands.

The hope for a premier wilderness in the East lay dormant for decades. Then, in the mid 1980s, it was rekindled and surfaced as a proposal put forth by George Davis, former executive director of the Adirondack Council. This proposal called for combining existing state lands along with an earnest acquisition effort to secure selected adjacent private parcels. A roadless area of up to half a million acres would thereby be created and the vision of Bob Marshall brought to fruition. Davis proposed also naming the new area after Marshall as both a compliment to the individual and as a fitting complement to the western

Bob Marshall Area. The area thus created would be expansive enough to assure viable populations of the extirpated megafauna and also ample enough to insure that mainly natural processes would regulate the heartbeat of its ecosystem.

In response to the above proposal, the DEC put forth the concept of an "Oswegatchie Great Forest." Their proposal envisioned protecting the three branches of the Oswegatchie River and most of their drainage basins in the area, plus the headwaters of the Bog and Beaver Rivers. The DEC's vision of the "Great Forest" is essentially the same as George Davis' with the exception of nomenclature.

Why the name switch? I don't know and quite frankly consider it unimportant. Perhaps apprehension at the confusion that could arise were there two similarly-named wildernesses in the same nation played an important part in the decision. The most significant thrust from all this is that something concrete has been put forth to preserve an area's wild essence which is unparalleled in the eastern part of our country; a last chance to protect an almost integral ecosystem in all its remaining parts: sterling forests, pristine ponds, free-flowing rivers, somber peatlands and all else that constitute the singular uniqueness of this area!

If there is one quality that best defines the Bob Marshall-Oswegatchie Forest as a whole it is that of an all-pervasive sense of wildness and remoteness. So overwhelming is this sense of the wild that it often appears to eclipse the many other wonders of Bob Marshall's paradise.

I have noticed that humans who penetrate the interior regions here are usually much better prepared for their sojourn than those who go to other wild areas of the Adirondacks. The High Peaks region springs immediately to mind. Relatively few get lost here and even fewer stay lost! In all my time here I can remember only two fatalities. One was a hunter who perished on Sitz Mountain in the western region of the Five Ponds Wilderness. The other was a hiker-backpacker who drowned while frolicking in the water at the foot of High Falls. Recreationists who trek into these remote reaches seem instinctively to sense the solitude and act accordingly.

My connection to this wilderness began with canoe hunting forays two decades ago. These forays up the Oswegatchie River from the Inlet put-in only occasionally resulted in the harvest of a white-tailed buck. They invariably, however, furnished that sense of inner peace and fulfillment that results only from a prolonged stay in a place blessed by the Deity. These stays of up to ten days at remote "Camp Johnny" and other entrancing sites along the river seemed to both soothe and rejuvenate my spirit from the battering it endured from police work in an urban metropolis.

Upon my retirement, it was my good fortune to be able to accompany one of the last truly authentic Adirondack guides on his wilderness trapping expeditions up the river. Red Johnson of Wanakena was the old guide's name and from him I absorbed much knowledge and forest lore. Truth be told, trapping was, in essence, an excuse for Red to sneak into the big green woods for weeks at a time. He did and I often accompanied him and treasure deeply those times today as much as I did then.

Beginning work on the original edition of ADK's *Guide to Adirondack Trails: Northern Region* was the next step in the process of acquiring an intimate knowledge of the "Bob." The knowledge started with the intimacy garnered in both walking and writing about the numerous miles of trails that wind their way through the backcountry. Some of these trails were truly of wilderness vintage, both in the remote regions they traversed and in their frequently hazy obscurity.

Canoeing and participation in the New York State Breeding Bird Census further heightened my awareness of and intimacy with the area. Some of the Breeding Bird Quadrants I surveyed were among the few in the entire state that had not a single road of any description in the tens of thousands of acres they encompassed. These were, of necessity, backpacking jaunts. Just me and the birds and, of course, the blackflies and deerflies.

The sense of solitude in this wilderness often obscures all else. After a period of adjustment to this solitude, the individual wonders of the area begin to emerge. Make no mistake about it, these natural gems of the Five Pond Wilderness are both sparkling and numerous.

The majestic and verdant old-growth forest perhaps most dramatically defines the area's wonders. These wonders usually become evident in a decidedly gradual and subtle fashion. Still, these remnants of a primeval and natural New York tend to dominate the senses of all who become acquainted with them. Continual discoveries are revealing the true depths of the intricate complexity of these old-growth ecosystems along with their bewildering biological relationships. The sense of wonder and awe imparted here to a lover of the natural is truly profound. So deep is it that the other glories of the Five Ponds-Oswegatchie Forest tend to be overlooked by someone who penetrates the interiors of these old-growth or "virgin" forest tracts.

There are two main areas of old-growth here. The larger one, encompassing 47,000+ acres, lies generally south of High Falls and extends to the shores of Stillwater Reservoir. Apparently this is the most extensive tract of old-growth forest in the entire northeastern United States. The tract was severely impacted by the hurricane of November 1950 and by the July 1995 microburst, but still retains numerous areas of regal-sized trees.

New York State came into ownership of this unique parcel in ironic fashion: as a result of the settlement of a lawsuit. In the 1890s the owners of the tract brought suit against the state of New York, claiming that the erection of a dam across the Beaver River to form Stillwater Reservoir had effectively isolated his parcel and rendered them unable to harvest the timber. The court agreed with the owners, the wealthy Webb family, and decreed that the state must now purchase the land from the Webbs. As a result of this fortunate happening, the people of the state of New York came into possession of this unrivaled treasure, thus protecting it for posterity.

The smaller of the two main areas of old-growth is comprised mostly of huge hardwoods and totals some 4,000 acres in extent. Located entirely in St. Lawrence County, it rolls across low ridges and knolls from the vicinity of Big Otter Pond to Griffin Rapids on the Oswegatchie.

In addition to these two major parcels, a number of lesser tracts scattered through the forest have also never experienced lumbering. Especially notable here are old-growth remnants located adjacent to both Inlet Flow and Dead Creek Flow. While these smaller tracts are impressive in their own right and do possess some of the ecological processes endemic to old-growth functioning, it is only on the larger tracts, spanning thousands of acres rather than scores, that the full spectrum of ecological processes, including species inter-relationships, can proceed completely unhindered and free of unnatural restraints.

The somber silence and gloom that prevails in the interior is generally the first thing one notes when entering these forests. Noted almost as quickly is the fact that many of the forest monarchs are horizontal rather than vertical. This profusion of downed trees, adorned on top with a verdant carpet of moss, is indeed one of the defining characteristics of old-growth. The downed logs are in varying states of decay and often have a luxurious array of saplings growing on them. This provides for tree regeneration despite the generally prevailing shade and the rich carpet of leaves on the floor of the forest.

The pit-and-mound topography so much in evidence here also provides handy places for seed germination. These unique areas are created by the fall of one of the forest giants. As this is ultimately inevitable, so too is the presence of the "pits and mounds" that speak of their toppling. I never go to one of the true old-growth stands without seeing them much in evidence, usually with a host of yellow birch seedlings on the mounds. These mounds, in addition, provide an ideal site for the regeneration of ferns and forbs of various hues and consequently are usually covered with a low blanket of green.

The fall of these trees from a mixture of storm, fire, and disease has created a tapestry of natural openings of all sizes in the forest. In these openings a variety of trees of the early successional or pioneer forest can be found spiraling for the open sky. White birch, aspen, and pin cherry are among them. The increased floral diversity also ultimately promotes a corresponding increase in faunal diversity.

Many of the standing trees, particularly the conifers, have their branches adorned with usnea moss, actually a variety of lichen. Almost tropical in aspect, usnea presents an eerie appearance as it is festooned from all the main branches of certain conifers. I often note it in tamarack, especially when they are adjacent to peatlands. If caribou were present in the Adirondacks in historical times, as many scientists are now stating, this lichen was almost certainly one of their major foods.

A sea of green appears to bracket the floor of the forest, despite the presence of unyielding shade. Sparse in diversity because of this shade, the relatively few species that can survive here are abundant in the number of individuals. Prominent shrubs are hobblebush (constantly tripping the unwary), red elder (with striking purple buds in evidence in winter), and fly honeysuckle. Closer to the ground, a variety of wood ferns, club moss, and various flowering herbs keep company with them.

As for smaller trees, the green bark of striped maple and the scarlet berries of mountain ash often seem to be present. The maple furnishes succulent leaves for deer and moose to browse on and also irresistible bark for bucks and bulls to rub on. On three separate occasions I have noticed moose using the bark of striped maple as rubs: quite impressive considering the current sparse population of Adirondack moose! The mountain ash serves up fruit for robins and evening grosbeaks as well as cedar waxwings. Several times I have watched hermit thrush gorge on the berries completely impervious to my presence only a few rods away.

The forest giants themselves differ widely in attributes, according to the individual tree species. White pine is the undisputed emperor, occasionally reaching a height of 160 feet as they tower over the mature under-canopy surrounding them. Scattered trees approaching this size can be seen across from the Inlet Flow in Wanakena. They can be reached by a bushwhack of no more that a quarter mile. To see trees of this stature in any number, however, it is necessary to go to Pine Ridge, a spot on the Oswegatche River several miles above High Falls. This stand was severely hurt by the hurricane of 1950, yet enough noble specimens remain standing today to satisfy the sense of awe of any lover of the wonderful.

Having a deep taproot, white pine is seldom uprooted entirely by the area's occasionally severe prevailing westerlies. More often they are snapped off, leaving a standing bole remaining for years as mute testimony to the velocity of the particular wind storm. While standing and during the many decades it takes to decay upon falling, the bole and log become an important and integgral part of the forest ecosyste.

I know today of pine snags of up to one hundred feet tall sprinkled through the forest. These snags may stand as ghostly hulks for scores of years before finally toppling. During all this time they furnish dens and retreats for a veritable menagerie of wildlife. I have seen use of these snags by bobcat, raccoon, fisher, marten, and flying squirrel. Gray fox are also thought to den here, and black bear are reputed to utilize these snags as hibernation sites during winter. I have not noticed that in the Adirondacks, however. Our Adirondack winter weather might simply be too frigid for that to occur!

Pileated woodpeckers seem to find these standing snags a paradise, judging from the abundance of their large rectangular holes. These holes are excavated by the woodpeckers as they seek the large black carpenter ants that dwell inside the trees. I often see the snags used as nesting sites and occasional roosts by the barred owl, our most common nocturnal raptor. Usually the unused nest of a red-tailed hawk is usurped for the occasion!

Hemlock, although not attaining the lofty heights of white pine, often exceeds it in girth and may reach an age in excess of five hundred years. This is by far the maximum in longevity attained by any Adirondack tree. Specimens of this caliber may be seen along the Peavine Creek Trail in the Cranberry Lake Wild Forest and also along the Dog Pond Loop. Porcupines browsing this tree in winter send the severed twigs cascading to the forest floor, where they provide white-tailed deer with much needed supplemental protein. Only once have I come upon a deer actually feeding on the fallen branches. With a piercing snort he bounded away into the frigid winter day.

Old-growth red spruce attains neither the height of white pine nor the girth of hemlock, but is still quite impressive in its own right. From my observations, one hundred feet appears to be the size limit reached locally. Some of these "virgin" spruce can be seen on the esker on the trail to Five Ponds and Sand Lake, although quite recently much of this stand has been ravaged by causes mostly unexplained. Acid precipitation, in combination with other factors, is widely believed to be the catalyst triggering this mortality. Whatever the reason, it is certainly a cause for much sadness to see the slow succumbing of these ancient trees. The ridge encircling Cage Lake also has a stand of accessible old-growth red spruce.

Old-growth hardwoods are distinctive in their own right. Hoary in aspect, the ancient ones all seem to acquire a grayish mantle to their outer bark as they start their slow succumbing to oblivion. This trait is evident in both sugar maple and yellow birch. In fact, as yellow birch achieves old age it sheds the smooth bark of its earlier years and superficially begins to resemble sugar maple. The hoary overall aspect of both makes them difficult to distinguish at first glance. Of the two, sugar maple is reputed to achieve the maximum longevity locally, up to 350 years or more. It is yellow birch, however, that reaches the ultimate in height of any Adirondack hardwood. I have seen one hundred-footers while I have heard reports of others that are even taller.

Wildlife dens are even more abundant in the hollows and cavities of old-growth hardwoods than they are in conifers. A sight ever treasured is that of a marten exiting from a hole in a twenty-foot sugar maple snag one frosty spring morning. This was especially memorable since the DEC was proposing reintroducing marten to the Five Ponds Wilderness, asserting with unswerving certitude that they did not currently reside there. My eyes widened somewhat and the first doubts concerning the infallibility of wildlife officialdom began to set in. Especially concerning what was and was not present in the remote reaches of the "Big Woods!"

My sightings of the more prosaic raccoon as they emerged from or entered some huge hollow hardwood near water are too numerous to recount entirely. The evidence is irrefutable: these hollow snags and logs are completely indispensable as habitat for almost all small and medium-sized predators of the forest. I would only exclude the aquatic otter and mink in this regard.

Another defining characteristic of the wilderness is the huge area sprawling generally south of High Falls which has remained totally bereft of trails of any sort. Although comparisons are difficult to make, this area could be the largest one without a trail in the entire Northeast. The exact size of the total area without trails is uncertain, but it appears to be at least 20,000 acres at a minimum. The very wildness of this area bespeaks another order entirely. Proper preparation, both physically and mentally, is an absolute necessity before entering it!

A trail was actually begun in this area in the 1920s, stretching north from Stillwater Reservoir. Noted conservationist A.T. Shorey laid the trail out for the then infant ADK. It followed closely the route of a rough hunters' path dating to the nineteenth century and known to local outdoorsmen as the "Fur, Fin and Feather Way."

When I arrived in the area a quarter century ago there were still old woodsmen who remembered this path with a positive gleam in their eye. Many were the wistful conversations that I had with them, conjuring up visages of hunting and trapping forays of long ago! No matter, this old path of the nimrod as well as the marked trail of A.T. Shorey, called officially the Red Horse Trail, has faded into oblivion today. Naught remains to remind of this bygone era; silence and solitude reign supreme. Few people have enough knowledge to penetrate through the area today. One who has done so a number of times is the now-retired DEC forest ranger stationed at Stillwater, Terry Perkins. It is not a trip to be recommended for the novice. Blowdown and beaver flooding are so pervasive that mere map and compass alone will not suffice. They will have to be supplemented by advanced woodsmanship and at least a slight measure of good luck!

After the forest and trees have finally been absorbed, the other wonders and delights of the Oswegatchie Great Forest slowly become apparent. Foremost are myriad sparkling ponds and lakes strewn over the landscape like beads in a necklace. These water bodies, all of glacial origin, are in fact a defining feature of the wilderness.

A hundred or so of these glacial gems bear names on the USGS topographic maps. Some are so remote and/or small that they remain unnamed unless they harbor a viable brook trout population. They range from large lakes that have been further increased in size by the erection of dams, to tiny ponds that' are mere dimples on the forest floor. All are unique and possess an aura of their very own. They differ in size, setting, and in the flora and fauna contained within and around them. They range from sprawling Cage Lake with its virgin conifers and loons to tiny Glasby Pond with its cut-over hardwoods and hooded mergansers. These bodies of water are deserving of a chapter of their own, and such I have given them. Many have been impacted by acid precipitation, but others still possess the delectable brook trout in abundance. Try as I might, I have never had any luck casting from the shores of these primeval ponds. To catch trout under these pines, an easily inflatable rubber raft is an absolute necessity!

Having their origin, also, in the abundant water resources with which this area is richly endowed are small creeks and waterfalls. The creeks are auxiliaries of the area's rivers and the waterfalls are scattered haphazardly around the forest.

The streams all contain varying populations of brook trout and their favorite food, stoneflies and mayflies. Watching the trout compete with cedar waxwings and yellow-rumped warblers in seizing them as they alight from the water to begin their adult life is, I have to admit, sheer ecstasy for me. Tamarack, Six Mile, and Bassett Creeks are particular favorites of mine. All have trout and their entire lengths, to nine miles, completely in the Forest Preserve, far from the nearest road.

The waterfalls are impressive in their own right, but not quite as spectacular as those on the South Branch of the Grass River where the Adirondack plateau begins its main descent into the St. Lawrence Valley. Still, these waterfalls all exhibit an undeniable charm of their very own. Most prominent among them is High Falls on the upper Oswegatchie in the town of Fine. Marked only by a modest descent, it nonetheless holds a place in local lore and legend far exceeding its plunge.

Around the turn of the century, sportsmen from all over the country gathered at Bert Dobson's camp there. They delighted in, among other things, the spectacle of six-pound native trout trying to jump over the falls in their autumn breeding frenzy.

Today, High Falls, though nestled as deep in the wilds as it was then, is a veritable Mecca in the wilderness. It is reached by both a popular hiking loop and an even more popular canoe route. Two lean-tos located here, often full on weekends, attest to its position as the most popular destination point in the Great Oswegatchie Forest. The hiker who recently perished at the foot of the falls also attests to the fact that proper preparation is still as essential now for a trip here as it was in earlier times.

Two other modest waterfalls are also noteworthy in the Bob Marshall Wilderness or Oswegatchie Great Forest. They also possess distinctive allures of their own. Possibly no more remote setting can be envisioned today than that occupied by one of the falls, Sliding Rock Falls. Five miles up the Robinson River, which is itself a remote tributary of the Oswegatchie above High Falls, this waterfall lies at the very heart of the trailless area.

Shortly after World War II an aircraft went down in a beaver meadow adjacent to the river a short distance below the falls. So remote is this site that the aircraft reposed here for two decades until discovered by an intrepid trout fisherman ascending the river one spring. The propellers of the aircraft were taken to a store owned by the local ranger, where they remained on display until pilfered by persons unknown. Considering the size of one propeller, as I recall it, a goodly number of these "persons unknown" were doubtlessly involved!

A cascade with a similar name, Sliding Falls, is found along Six Mile Creek at a relatively short distance from where it flows into the

South Flow of Cranberry Lake. Aside from the idyllic setting, its main attraction appears to be an appeal to individuals with suicidal tendencies (latent at least) who attempt to ride over its fifteen-foot drop in spring. The result usually entails a visit to Clifton-Fine Hospital in Star Lake for repairs.

Modest, too, are the low pinnacles that loom protectively over the area's rolling expanse of forest and swampland. This lack of height is more than balanced by the enchantment of wildness that pervades the setting. This wildness permeates the entire area and is dramatically underlined by the views from the pinnacles themselves. So characteristic of the Oswegatchie Great Forest are they that they share a chapter in this book along with the rivers and lakes of the region.

The diversity in these low peaks is best illustrated by a comparison of Cat Mountain with Partlow Mountain. What can be more different than trackless Partlow Mountain with old-growth forest mantling its slopes and summits, and Cat Mountain with its well-traversed trail, remnants of a fire tower and apple trees on top from the days of the fire tower? Yet both are indicative of the forest and typical in their own way.

The very name of Cat Mountain evokes images of mystery and wildness springing from the felines whose name it bears. I have on several occasions seen signs of bobcat while ascending the mountain and on one occasion a distinctive eerie feeling that I was being followed came over me. All this I recalled recently when a friend, a seasoned woodsperson, informed me that she and her companion had spied a cougar in broad daylight while descending the mountain. How fitting and now how more apt the name!

"Bob Marshall Wilderness," "Oswegatchie Great Forest"—call it what you may, it's out there wild and wondrous. Wondrous also is the mere knowledge that it exists! A cherished hope that I hold most dear is that the current efforts to protect these public and private wildlands and establish an official "Wilderness" will eventually bear fruit. For not only is this area too spectacular to lose but it is also the very core and soul of the Great South Woods.

XII

LEGEND AND LORE

Oswegatchie River

As the Great South Woods was not settled permanently until relatively late, the age of agriculture by and large passed it over. It nonetheless has an interesting reservoir of tales that speak of legend and lore. Unlike in most areas of New York State, the tales here are mainly concerned with hunting and fishing from the earliest times until the present. Tales of early lumbering of the virgin forest and logging as it exists today also play a major role in local legend and lore.

189

Some of the early woodsmen and would-be entrepreneurs had an impact so powerful that their presence seems to resonate in the area to this very day. They indeed seem, at times, to be an indelible part of the process of these forests, waters, and mountains. The truly discerning can actually "feel" their memory! They are already a part of legend.

There are others I have encountered in my forest travels whom I feel will one day assume this mantle. Their impression will grade imperceptibly into the fabric of the forest and they too will become part of the legacy of the Great South Woods. For today, however, they remain in the realm of lore.

BERT DOBSON and HIS ELEGANT SPORTSMAN'S CAMP

High Falls today is situated at a crossroads of wilderness trails, a mecca for both the hiker and canoeist. All now is serene and placid with only the whisper of the wind and the cries of the woodland denizens to interrupt the timeless march of the seasons. Until the microburst of July 1995 descended so dramatically in the area, an uninterrupted canopy of pines and hardwoods loomed protectively upon the falls and lean-tos nestled beneath them. The area has been altered considerably by the impact of that storm. One who flew over the devastation was heard to utter a remark relative to the lean-tos now being the tallest things standing within sight. So much for anything being timeless and impervious to change!

But the area has witnessed change before—and change of a somewhat draconian nature. This isolated forest crossroads played host at the turn of the last century to a rustic sporting camp that was renowned throughout the entire eastern United States. Bert Dobson ran it and to it flocked seekers of sport and solitude from near and far. The scenery was stunning; the tranquillity a tonic for the soul, and above all the sport of the chase gave thrills and ecstasy beyond description to the fortunate clients of Bert Dobson.

Among those of note who graced the camps with their presence were Ernest Thompson Seton, Irving Bacheller, Frederic Remington, and a host of lesser luminaries. The hunting of deer and black bear with packs of hounds lured some, while for others the more subtle wonders of the wilderness surroundings were the chief appeal. The spectacle of four-pound native brook trout trying to leap up the cascade at the falls was a view cherished by many admirers. The leap was invariably futile, but this did not deter in the least these ambitious trout.

Bert Dobson cut his own trail from Wanakena to High Falls. Running almost due south, it existed as a hazy, unmarked footpath for woodsmen in the know until the microburst of July 15, 1995, arrived. The path is now pretty much obliterated, but as is the way of the woods a time may come again for the Dobson Trail.

I fondly recall Red Johnson of Carthage, New York, one of the last of the old-time woodsmen, informing me of how in his younger days he and a companion would leave High Falls for a dance in Wanakena and return to the falls after the dance the same night. This was while they were guiding sportsmen just before the Depression. The route they used was the Dobson Trail.

In Bert Dobson's day many of the big pines had been cut. New ones subsequently grew back to a noble size as the twentieth century wound its course. With the devastation unleashed by the microburst, it would appear that nature has come full circle in this wilderness crossroads.

INLET HOUSE and the OLD ALBANY ROAD

This was the site of another hotel catering to sportsmen. The Inlet House, located at a ford on the Oswegatchie River, was far more substantial than Dobson's rustic camp. In addition to an extensive vegetable garden, the Inlet House also kept cows for fresh milk. Guests were taken by motorboat up the Oswegatchie River on hunting and fishing forays until 1963, when the buildings and adjacent lands were sold to the state of New York.

The Albany Road crossed the Oswegatchie at this ford, for this is in fact the first practical crossing of the river below its headwaters. The Albany Road follows the route of an Indian path which the loyalist William Johnson's family utilized when fleeing their lands in the Mohawk Valley to safety in Canada during the American Revolution.

Over a generation after Johnson's flight, the state legislature authorized the construction of a military turnpike along this route to terminate near the town of Russell. The War of 1812 was a catalyst for construction and work commenced around this time. Construction was piecemeal and sporadic so that it is doubtful if any vehicle ever traversed the entire length of the road. The path can still be detected in places; I recall an old wooden sign denoting the roadway still being in existence in 1991. I recall also the ancient cannons, relics of Sir William Johnson's hasty sojourn along the route, which were recovered earlier in the century.

The site where the road crossed the river apparently was always a magnet for human activities. It is one of the few places in the Adirondack Park where Indian arrowheads and other like artifacts have been uncovered.

The road itself, now mainly a path, was used by early settlers from the town of Fine to reach areas along the Oswegatchie Plains and other brook marshes where they harvested wild hay for their domestic stock. This was when they first arrived in the region and had yet to cut the local virgin forests and plant their own pastures and fields.

The area is today an official canoe launching area for the trek up the Oswegatchie. The aura of the past is still heavily felt. I detected it immediately even though I did not become acquainted with the locale until almost a decade after the old buildings had been razed. The hotel had a number of owners over the generations, but the ones who left their imprint most firmly attached were the Sternbergs, who were the pioneers. Old woodsmen say that it is their aura which lingers so powerfully today.

BIG DEER POND and the EMPEROR of the WOODS

Big Deer Pond is an expansive, shallow lake noted for the ubiquity of white-tailed deer that seem forever to be prancing in its waters and on its shores. It lies nestled deep within the Five Ponds Wilderness far from the haunts of man. Yet this remote woodland loch was the setting for a novel that achieved national success at the turn of the twentieth century.

The novel was *Silas Strong – Emperor of the Woods,* by the Canton-born Irving Bacheller. Silas Strong was based on an actual local woodsman whose character, if anything, was even more colorful than that of the one portrayed in the novel. Fido Scott, of the town of Fine, was one of the itinerant hunter-trappers who proliferated in the area around this time. Called Uncle Fide by the local children, with whom he was quite popular, Fido resided at Scott's Bridge on the Oswegatchie River during the down months of the winter. Come April, and the scene changed dramatically for Fido. For at this time he took his cow Betsy and loaded her with enough supplies to survive in the woods for seven months. He then commenced an eight-mile journey through the forest to the shores of Big Deer Pond. His dog and cat followed dutifully and together they made up a slightly different version of the nuclear family. But family they were, ensconced snugly at Big Deer Pond until just before Thanksgiving.

Fido utilized an abandoned lumber camp at Big Deer as his headquarters. The extremely shallow depth of the lake precluded any substantial population of brook trout, but shoreline waters were quite another matter. The many aquatic plants and their high sodium level had a positively magnetic attraction for white-tailed deer.

Fido and his entourage (except for Betsy) survived on venison for their entire stay. Fido harvested no more than he needed to sustain himself for the seven months. He appeared in fact to have some kind of arrangement with local guides by which he kept poachers at bay. This arrangement apparently also extended to the lumber company that owned all land in the vicinity of the pond before it was sold to the state. They winked at his annual "squatting" on their property in return for services rendered.

At length there came a time in November when the newly fallen white began not to melt off the ground so quickly. It was then time for Fido and his caravan to start their trek back to the settlements and their winter abode. I have searched long and hard, but the only remnants I could find that harken back to those long-ago days were some irregularities in the surface of the forest floor that indicated where the lumber camp once stood. That and the spirit of Uncle Fido, ever present.

ANDREW SHULER and HIS DOMAIN

It was a cool, gray day with the rains relentlessly cascading from the sky when a man with vision was laid to rest in an imposing mausoleum constructed of native pink granite gneiss. The locale was a remote setting overlooking a wild, sprawling Adirondack lake. The man was named Andrew Shuler and the lake was called Streeter.

Streeter Lake was named to honor a turn-of-the-century woodsman who left his mark in the woods. Of later years, however, the lake and its environs became intimately associated with the Shuler family. The family fortune had been made in potato chips and the vision of the man was to create a replica of an all-embracing fiefdom on the 5,000 acres which he owned in this wilderness.

A field of approximately one hundred acres was hacked out of the wilderness to plant seed potatoes to supply the family's extensive potato farms near Bath, New York. A remote site such as this would surely harbor no pernicious potato beetles to harass the crop! Exotic Norway spruce was liberally planted all along the perimeter of the potato field. They still exist, as does the old field providing a vivid contrast with the surrounding wilderness. The field's presence today owes its existence to the too-intensive plowing of the original virgin soils. This rapidly depleted soil nutrients and resulted in a permanent mantle of moss that has retarded the growth of herbs and trees.

Crystal Lake, just over a modest ridge from Streeter, was selected as the official swimming hole. Sand was transported from the vicinity of Niagara Falls to create a beach on its shore. Fourteen acres in size but up to ninety feet deep in places, Crystal Lake was famous in local lore for never having had any fish in its emerald green waters. Some chemicals in the water probably inhibited fish survival, much as they make swimming here much more effortless than in most Adirondack lakes. All this before the advent of acid precipitation! On a number of occasions I have spied loons on Crystal Lake but careful observation disclosed that all their diving and feeding concerned only crustaceans and aquatic insects.

Carlos Law, an expert woodsman, was installed as caretaker of this domain and some interesting occurrences then commenced. One of these was the live trapping of bobcat kits for sale to representatives of two circuses that appeared at Star Lake in early springtime. What remains of the cages used to hold and transport the bobcats prior to their sale remains strewn over the forest to this very day. I clearly remember the utter shock I experienced when I first came upon them while doing research for my first trail guide!

Then, too, there are tales of moose wandering into this domain in the 1960s and then utterly disappearing. Skeletal remains of two adults and a calf were discovered just before the state purchased Andy Shuler's domain in 1979. I was fortunate enough to see the splendid mansion and boathouse that stood on the shores of Streeter Lake before the state demolished them in 1980 in accordance with the legal mandate for the Forest Preserve. The telephone and electric wires that provided services to this remote location did not have to be similarly destroyed. They ran fully underground for five miles through the Forest Preserve before reaching what was then a large inholding in the midst of state land. Remnants of his underground wire can still be seen today when they sporadically come to the surface along the trail from Star Lake.

The one-acre mausoleum grounds are today managed as a cemetery and maintained by Clarkson University, to which Andrew Shuler donated his substantial fortune. Rows of potatoes are planted among the elegant sculpted garden that surrounds this resplendent memorial. I think it quite fitting an epitaph even though the potato plants are invariably browsed heavily by the voracious deer herd that exists here.

Today the entire area is an oasis of pastoral tranquillity reposing in the middle of the wilderness. It is heavily used by the public for recreation. A DEC lean-to lies on the shore of Streeter Lake and more often than not is occupied by a party of fishermen or hunters. Crystal Lake is now the swimming hole for a much more numerous and diverse clientele than it was in the days of Andrew Shuler's domain. My children and I spent many summer days there experiencing the delights of its mineral-laden, buoyant waters.

Somehow, I feel, Andrew Shuler, would be quite pleased if he could see what his once-private domain has become.

AUGUSTUS A. LOW and HIS DREAM

Of all the remnants of long-ago wilderness settlements that today lie deep in the Forest Preserve, none is more renowned regionally than the former empire of Augustus A. Low. Harkening back to an era when wilderness entrepreneurism was all the rage, many signs of this once-splendid domain remain to this very day.

The entrepreneur and architect of this wilderness enterprise was a scion of one of Brooklyn's original Dutch families. Born to wealth, he endeavored to accumulate even more by taming the forest primeval and harnessing it to produce tangible products and benefits. His thrift was neatly summed up in the adage "waste not, want not."

Low loved the wilderness, as was the fashion then very much in vogue. That fashion dictated that the wilderness be managed intensively, mostly to accrue financial benefits. A sort of sylvan agriculture is what came to prevail.

Accordingly, Low set about exploiting his entire 40,000 acres for this purpose. In 1896 he built a private railroad station at Horseshoe Lake solely for the transportation of his family and the products of his enterprise. He then constructed dams at two different locations across the Bog River in 1903 and 1907. Henceforth, he had his own source of power to fuel his enterprise.

He began by intensively yet scientifically harvesting the timber on the tracts. Mills and other buildings were erected for this purpose. He next turned his endeavors to maple syrup from the abundant sugar maple trees that thrived locally. At peak production, 20,000 gallons of delicious maple syrup was shipped for the enjoyment of customers all over the Northeast.

The abundant local water supply was then targeted. Springs were tapped and a supply of pure, fresh spring water was extracted from the water table and shipped to areas as far away as Boston and New York.

All these endeavors have faded into the realm of history, yet much remains that is tangible even to this day. A large, sprawling house still stands (as of 1995) on the shores of Hitchins Pond. Gutted and dilapidated in the extreme, it is now a mere skeleton giving testimony to the past. I recall hundreds of dead bats littered over the entire inner portions of the building.

The house has a most unique history. Originally it housed the lumberjacks who harvested the forest for Low. From a lodging house it became the primary abode of the Low family and was duly improved as such. Finally, after the sale of the property to the Boy Scouts, the old building became the main dormitory for them in summer. The stories it could tell!

The two dams across the Bog River also remain and are an integral part of the Bog River Canoe Route. In fact, without them the canoe route would be more dream than reality.

On the steep, bald-faced ridge looming above the old boarding house, an iron plaque commemorating Augustus A. Low is imbedded into the bare rock. This gives a good reason to climb the ridge, along with the view of the entire Bog River Valley.

The Low family had a string of German shepherds and duly erected metal plaques over all their remains when they passed on. The memorial stood right at the canoe landing on Hitchins Pond. Since the canoe route was opened to the public, however, vandals have removed all the inscribed metal plaques from the cement pillars holding them in place.

Another interesting aspect of Augustus Low's domain was the existence of the Broadhead Gore and its final disposition. The gore was an irregularity in the southern boundary line of St. Lawrence County that ran for more than eight miles through the heart of the wilderness. Varying from several hundred feet to several hundred yards wide, it was considered state land and posted as Forest Preserve until Augustus Low brought a lawsuit against New York State in the 1940s, claiming the land in question belonged to him. He won the case and promptly logged the virgin forest before selling the land to the Boy Scouts. The second-growth forest that has subsequently regrown here was quite distinctive from the remaining old growth surrounding it until the microburst of 1995 acted as a general leveler of all in sight.

Today all in sight is also part of the Forest Preserve. This is quite ironic considering the apparent manner in which Augustus Low viewed public recreation on his domain. Now, however, the public is permitted to participate in and enjoy the glories and splendor once reserved for the affluent elite. This is as it should be despite the occasional petty pilfering of canine memorials and such by a wayward few.

BARNEY BURNS and the STONE CHIMNEY

It stands today, forlorn yet defiant in the midst of the wild shores of Brandy Brook Flow on Cranberry Lake. It is quite a contrast to the wild, and of course has quite a tale behind it as well. I first encountered it while researching my first *Guide to Adirondack Trails: Northern Region* and thereafter never ceased to be stunned no matter how often I came upon it while traversing the trail to Dog Pond.

The twenty-foot stone chimney originally belonged to a resplendent, elite sportsmen's club located on Indian Mountain Pond high on the slopes of Indian Mountain. The club had erected an extravagant clubhouse on the shores of the tiny pond and the elaborately sculpted stone chimney was the centerpiece of their luxurious abode. The chimney came into the possession of renowned guide and hunter Barney Burns when New York State purchased the lands of the Indian Mountain Club and incorporated them into the Forest Preserve.

The original setting of Barney Burns' camp had been a rough hewn three-sided shelter open to the elements in front. This was to be the precursor and the prototype of the famed Adirondack lean-to and Barney Burns was among the first to use it in this entire region.

When he came into possession of the chimney, Barney built a far more substantial edifice for the many clients he attracted from all over the East. These clients included a number of prominent personages among their number. Among the luminaries who kept returning were Ernest Thompson Seton and the renowned artist Frederic Remington. Remington had been born in St. Lawrence Country, but subsequently migrated West where he achieved national fame through his artistic depictions of the frontier and prairies.

Barney Burns possessed an unparalleled reputation as a nimrod, or mighty hunter. The native brook trout still reigned supreme, and the cool waters of Brandy Brook harbored some of the more mammoth of these virgin brook trout. Hence those in pursuit of finned wildlife were also delighted. Add to this the fact that the hounding of deer with dogs was still legal at the beginning of Barney's tenure in these forests and it readily becomes apparent why he was so often able to fulfill his claim that his clients were assured of trophy deer. Barney reigned supreme here as long as the game was good and he was unhindered by advanced age.

Although that era is now long past, much of the ambiance remains to this day. The aura of yesterday is heightened by the presence of a curious anomaly along the shores of Brandy Brook Flow. This is the existence of a number of houseboats functioning as rustic "camps" moored to the adjoining shoreline. Trespassers all, they have with the passage of time been deemed legal if they do not actually touch shore. Cynics say they seem to be proliferating in both style and quantity.

All of the above lends a most distinctive aura to the area—one that at times can be palpably felt—a feeling that Barney or some of his clients or both are observing all. Maybe they are!

THE OVER-THE-HILL GANG

They once proudly hailed themselves as the "River Rats." From all parts of the Northeast they came, seemingly from time immemorial, to canoe and hunt the upper reaches of the Oswegatchie River. Actually it was only from the 1930s onward that they gathered at the landing site at Inlet to launch their expedition into the remote Five Ponds Wilderness, but their tenure here seemed to be infinite.

Then the Oswegatchie was declared a "wild river" in 1973 and conditions changed radically. Motors were henceforth banned on the river and the gas-fired engines that the "Over-the-Hill Gang" used to propel their canoes and other craft were now to be a thing of the past. As the years had advanced significantly on many of their members, they stoically resigned themselves to reality and altered their plan of access to the wilderness. From now on their point of assembly was to be Janack's Landing on Dead Creek Flow, which was still within the reach of motorized boats. Here they set up base camp every autumn and conducted their hunting forays into the interior.

It was an exceedingly warm, desultory October afternoon when I first encountered them. For all practical purposes, the weather had made the pursuit of white-tailed deer pointless and so I dropped over Round Top Mountain to the "Plains" below, doing more nature observing than hunting. There my path met with three of the former River Rats. Now styling themselves the "Over-the-Hill Gang" in recognition of the new order of things, they were trekking on the old Plains Trail on their way back to the camp on Dead Creek Flow.

After an initial conversational greeting, I received a gracious invite back to base camp for coffee from the trio and I gratefully accepted. Back in the substantial, enclosed canvas tent that served as their base camp, I proceeded to bring up a topic close to my heart over the delightful aroma of forest-brewed coffee. Who else, I figured, would have as intimate a knowledge of those extirpated "creatures of the shadow" as a group such as this? To my query about cougars, they stated that none of them had ever seen one, but that a few times over the years members of other hunting parties had purported to have spied one of these feline creatures of mystery. Allegedly one had even been shot at in the 1950s by a member of one of these parties.

They next solemnly produced a faded, hard-bound log chronicle that recorded in meticulous fashion the details and results of every annual hunting trip from World War II on. The log chronicle, resembling the desk blotter I used as a New York City Police Sergeant, left very little of the essentials unrecorded. It detailed among other matters the daily weather patterns, listed all present, and recorded all big game harvested. This included a smattering of black bear and bobcat among the myriad white-tailed deer taken over the years.

Among all these official items there was recorded a detailed account of an encounter with a wolverine that no fewer than three members of the hunting party purportedly had in 1963. The animal was vividly described as were the circumstances of the sighting. All was then duly transcribed into their "official" log. The members present that day of my visit had a completely satisfied glow on their countenances regarding the incident. After all, cougars are seen by not a few in the Adirondacks, but a wolverine!

I admit to being quite perplexed and to have pondered the matter in great detail. Subsequently I heard of other claimed sightings of this king of the mustelids locally. A pair of friends and competent woodsmen reported one near Aldrich and another incident involving one at the West Canada Lake Ranger Station was relayed to me by a forest ranger. As implausible as these accounts may at first appear, they are no more so than some of the other mysteries hidden in the forested folds of the Great South Woods.

Although I am at a loss to explain the matter, my thoughts of late often turn to the Over the Hill Gang, and their wolverine!

TRAPP CAMP

It was the most rustic of deer camps, much used and much loved. It was nestled under a towering canopy of white pine and northern hardwoods by the banks of the upper Oswegatchie.

To this sylvan retreat came for decades the same Trapp family party, who obtained a permit from the local forest ranger to erect a tarp shelter permitted to stand for the duration of the hunting season. So intense and profuse was the affection this family had for their temporary "little bit of heaven" in the Forest Preserve that they even seeded a grassy area between their tent site and the banks of the river! Here good times galore were had in abundance. The aura of prey harvested as well as prey that outwitted its pursuers is still redolent in the air today and can be sensed by a visitor to that remote spot.

The good times here, like good times everywhere, at length came to an end. The end, however, came about in a sudden and tragic manner.

After a day of hard hunting, one of the members of the party was in the process of unloading his rifle just outside the tent when he inadvertently discharged a bullet that struck and immediately killed the mentor of the family, who was inside the tent. After this tragedy, the camp was completely abandoned by the family, who even left some of their equipment behind in their haste to depart.

The incident gradually assumed the mantle of legend on the Oswegatchie and for years local woodsmen and guides scrupulously avoided the site. The old potbelly stove and other equipment slowly slumbering and rusting away under the pines added to the haunted aura that pervaded here.

The most vivid memory I retain of the site is a rain-drenched summer evening when a companion and I pitched a tent here to seek respite from the torrential downpour engulfing us. Later, after we had setup camp, I happened to mention the history of the site to him. He abruptly left the tent and proceeded to paddle the canoe another quarter-mile upriver under a canopy of unrelenting rainfall. Then he found his night's rest at a spot on the shore, in the open. It was probably inertia more than anything else that prohibited me from following him. To the best of my recall my slumber went completely unencumbered that evening. If there were any visits from spectral spirits, they have long been consigned to the forgotten memories of the Oswegatchie.

When my companion returned in the morning not a word was mentioned of the previous night's happenings under the clouds. We enjoyed our oatmeal amidst the dew and pretended the events listed above had never occurred. So we pretend to this very day!

SAM'S CURVE

There it stood, perched on the banks of the Oswegatchie River three miles or so from the Inlet landing in a setting as similar to the boreal taiga of Alaska as anything in the "Lower 48." It certainly was an anachronism here, a plain white wooden sign mounted on a five-foot post proclaiming the simple words "Sam's Curve" in the midst of wilderness.

It had stood for over a generation in this remote venue, perplexing countless paddlers as they rounded a sharp bend in the river. What, if anything, did the sign attest to? As the story unfurled like a leaf in springtime, it seems that the sign in question did most definitely attest to something. Therein lies a tale unique to the Oswegatchie.

The original events in question had transpired long enough ago to be as obscure as the river itself when shrouded in the morning mists. A good deal of probing was required to dispel these mists and bring the epic of Sam to the surface.

Sam was one of a party of downstaters who made repeated trips to the Oswegatchie country in pursuit of the fabled white-tailed deer and native brook trout. These expeditions appeared to commence during the Great Depression and were a regular annual occurrence. Sam himself seemed by all accounts to be a particularly avid enthusiast of the deep green forests and waterways of this section of the Great South Woods.

One fatal autumn day, so the tale goes, Sam met his demise through drowning after falling out of his motor boat while making the sharp turn here. A certain segment of tradition also claims that Sam had imbibed too freely before his fall, but this is disputed by others. Be that as it may, what is definite is that Sam's grieving comrades erected the sign in his memory at the site of the fatality.

In the early 1970s the Oswegatchie River was officially declared a Wild River, as noted elsewhere in this book. In addition to banning all motors on the river, this also had the effect of banning all "non-conforming structures" from the river's banks. Sam's sign was most assuredly this, making it illegal.

Due primarily to the remote locale of the setting, things pretty much remained status quo for over a decade after the official proclamation. All this ended, however, when noted environmentalist and member of the APA, Peter Paine, spied the nonconforming structure while making the Oswegatchie-Bog River Canoe Trek. He duly notified the APA and the local DEC forest ranger was instructed to remove the illegal sign. This he reluctantly did and a sign proclaiming Sam's Curve was now absent from the secluded river setting for the first time in over three decades.

Lo and behold, as nature abhors a vacuum so too did the site not remain bereft of a sign for any length of time. Two months later, while leisurely paddling upriver, I spied a brand new sign at the site—an even larger sign, but one adorned in the environmentally friendly earth colors of the DEC that stated to all who viewed it that this was indeed Sam's Curve. While probably still illegal, it was less at variance with the wilderness background of its location.

I came away with two thoughts from this episode. One was that the comrades of Sam possessed a strong sense of loyalty to him. The other was that they also possessed a sense of humor.

FLOWER LADY

The year was 1985. She arrived like the morning dew following a chilly night. One day she was just there, at the old sand pit just a little ways down the Dead Creek Flow Truck Trail. Actually, I subsequently learned that she solicited a ride from Tupper Lake with a local couple who were somewhat embarrassed by it as events unfolded.

She remained encamped at the old sand pit, month after month, as the Adirondack springtime progressed into high summer. That plague of torment that tortures normal woodspeople, blackflies, appeared to present no undue problemue problem to disdaining to arm herself with any insect repellent, she seemed to be completely impervious to their vile attention. She was clad in a light cotton dress (the same one through the months) with bare arms and legs and possessed neither a sleeping bag nor tent.

Thus she persisted, waving her arms constantly and frantically at the insect hordes that buzzed incessantly around her. All the while she yelled the choicest invective and imprecations at her "tiny winged tormentors." It seemed to me a standoff, but I imagine she felt she was prevailing in her persistence to remain at the spot.

She provided for her meager wants by keeping volumes of flour in a trunk she trundled into the woods with her. Once a week she replenished these sparse supplies by traipsing into Wanakena and shopping at the one store there. A brilliantly colored flower invariably adorned her grayish brown hair. Because of it and the supply of flour that created her victuals I applied the moniker of "Flower Lady" to her person when discussing her with a small circle of local woodsfolk. It was especially meaningful as she adamantly refused to divulge her name to anyone who spoke to her.

I became acquainted with her as I was researching the Five Ponds Wilderness trails for inclusion in the first edition of my northern Adirondack trail guide for ADK. A stout woman, I presumed her to be about my age (forty-six at the time), but I found she was actually only thirty-nine when she consented to reveal her age (but not her name).

She informed me on a number of occasions that she was waiting here at this spot in the Five Ponds Wilderness to have a rendezvous with her husband, Carl. She further stated upon my inquiring that Carl told her to go here in a dream in which he came to her. I now knew I was in the presence of a being of a different order. I admit to becoming a little solicitous and sort of watching out that no harm befell her. She seemed not to need any help from me whatsoever, though, as she kept thriving, apparently without much effort at this most inhospitable of sites.

One day she suddenly asked me out of the blue if I was a policeman. When I queried her as to how she knew, she replied that I resembled Carl, who was also one. I then asked the question that had been vexing me for a while: Where was Carl right now? When she stated matter of factly that he had died five years ago I knew that occasionally, at least, sheer lunacy could become entwined with elements of a higher existence.

All the while the local forest rangers, who were concerned for her safety, were making efforts to get her to leave her sylvan abode. Ill-equipped as she apparently was, they regretted issuing her a permit to camp in the Forest Preserve and were not renewing it.

Finally they seemed to prevail. One day she suddenly was not there. Like the dew being evaporated by the midday sun, she simply disappeared. To where or why is unknown to this day. I never pass the old sand pit without reflection on the tenure here of the Flower Lady. And, of course, whether she and Carl ultimately had their meeting!

POSTSCRIPT

Photo courtesy of Betsy Tisdale

Cranberry Lake

As with many literary efforts, there has been a moderate interval of time between the writing and publication of this book. During that interval there were significant developments in several of the topics covered. Among the most noteworthy were the following:

1) Champion Lands: The entire 30,000 acre tract of land along the Tooley Pond Road has now been officially transferred to New York State in a fee/easement combination. This opens up eighteen miles of

the South Branch of the Grass River as well as Tooley Pond Mountain.

2) The Mount Arab fire tower: The Friends of Mt. Arab have completed a refurbishing of the fire observer's cabin, as well as restoring access to the tower itself which now, once again, can be climbed. Plans are proceeding apace for an educational display outlining the history of New York State fire fighting and for a natural history display at the scene.

3) Wild turkey: The re-establishment of wild turkey range has continued at an accelerating pace. Turkey are now thriving in the most boreal areas of the region: Cranberry Lake, Sabbatis, and Wanakena, seemingly only minimally affected by the rigors of winter.

4) Elk: The Rocky Mountain Elk Foundation contracted out studies to SUNY ESF and to Cornell University to determine the feasibility of elk restoration in New York State. The studies concluded that the area encompassed in the Great South Woods possessed the best elk habitat in the state but also stated that the local towns did not have the *infrastructure* to achieve maximum benefit from any elk restoration. Consequently, an area in the Catskills was selected for consideration for any initial elk restoration in New York. Public hearings are progressing, at the time of this update (Summer 2000). Hopefully, the initiative will be extended to our area next with the backing of some local towns.

5) Wolf: The Washington, D.C. based Defenders of Wildlife, through a Citizens' Advisory Board of which I was a member, commissioned the Conservation Biology Institute of Corvallis, Oregon to undertake a biological feasibility study in furtherance of re-introducing wolves to the Adirondack Park. This study concluded that wolves would, in fact, survive for up to a century in the Adirondacks but would ultimately die out due to isolation from any currently existing wolf population in Canada.

I strongly dissented from this conclusion as did a number of other committee members including noted canid expert Dr. John Green, professor emeritus, St. Lawrence University. The study blatantly ignored the fact that several wolves have already been confirmed in the Adirondacks, as well as ignoring the Algonquin to Adirondack initiative that is being inaugurated to establish a wildlife corridor between the Adirondacks and Algonquin Park in Ontario. This was especially disappointing as the Cornell University sociological survey disclosed surprising support for the wolf throughout New York State and, to a lesser degree, even in the Adirondacks.

The study further stated that the wolf primarily present in the Adirondacks in the past was the red wolf with the gray wolf being found only sparingly. It recommended further studies and analysis to determine if the Adirondack canid present today is, in fact, a hybrid of the red wolf and coyote. The study also issued a number of recommendations that could pave the way for wolf restoration in the region at some time in the future.

The next step in the process will be the official U.S. Fish and Wildlife Recovery Plan for the entire Northeast. This plan is contingent, however, on local NYS DEC approval before moving forward. From my assessment of the attitude of the local Fish and Wildlife Division of the NYS DEC (as of early Spring 2000), I am not overly optimistic in this regard. Perhaps some new faces will allow hope to spring eternal that we will once again commonly hear the wolf howl in the Great South Woods.

INDEX